The True Meaning of Life

"*...as* **He** *is, so are* **we** *in this world.*"
I JOHN 4:17 (KJV)

GOD HAS BIG PLANS FOR YOU!

KYLE J. SHIRLEY, SR.

TRILOGY
A WHOLLY OWNED SUBSIDIARY OF TBN
PROFESSIONAL PUBLISHING MEETS POWERFUL PROMOTION

The True Meaning of Life

Trilogy Christian Publishers
A Wholly Owned Subsidiary of Trinity Broadcasting Network
2442 Michelle Drive, Tustin, CA 92780

Copyright © 2024 by Kyle J. Shirley Sr.

Scripture quotations marked AMP are taken from the Amplified® Bible. Copyright © 2015 by The Lockman Foundation. Used by permission. www.Lockman.org. All rights reserved.

Scripture quotations marked AMPC are taken from the Amplified® Bible, Classic Edition. Copyright © 1954, 1958, 1962, 1964, 1965, 1987 by The Lockman Foundation. Used by permission. www.lockman.org. All rights reserved.

Scripture quotations marked ASV are taken from the American Standard Version®. Copyright © 2019 by Thomas Nelson and Sons. Public domainwww.biblegateway.com. Used by permission. All rights reserved.

Scripture quotations marked TLB are taken from The Living Bible. Copyright ©1971. Used by permission of Tyndale House Publishers, a Division of Tyndale House Ministries, Carol Stream, Illinois 60188. All rights reserved.

Scripture quotations marked NASB are taken from the New American Standard Bible®. Copyright © 1960, 1962, 1963, 1968, 1971, 1972, 1973, 1975, 1977, 1995 by The Lockman Foundation. Used by permission. www.Lockman.org.

All Scripture quotations, unless otherwise noted, taken from THE HOLY BIBLE, NEW INTERNATIONAL VERSION®, NIV® Copyright © 1973, 1978, 1984, 2011 by Biblica, Inc.® Used by permission. All rights reserved worldwide.

Scripture quotations marked NKJV are taken from the New King James Version®. Copyright © 1982 by Thomas Nelson. Used by permission. All rights reserved.

Scripture quotations marked (KJV) taken from The Holy Bible, King James Version. Cambridge Edition: 1769.

All rights reserved, including the right to reproduce this book or portions thereof in any form whatsoever. For information, address Trilogy Christian Publishing Rights Department, 2442 Michelle Drive, Tustin, CA 92780.

Trilogy Christian Publishing/ TBN and colophon are trademarks of Trinity Broadcasting Network.

For information about special discounts for bulk purchases, please contact Trilogy Christian Publishing.

Trilogy Disclaimer: The views and content expressed in this book are those of the author and may not necessarily reflect the views and doctrine of Trilogy Christian Publishing or the Trinity Broadcasting Network.

10 9 8 7 6 5 4 3 2 1
Library of Congress Cataloging-in-Publication Data is available.

ISBN 979-8-89333-572-9
ISBN 979-8-89333-573-6 (ebook)

ACKNOWLEDGMENTS

Above all, I thank my Lord and savior, Jesus Christ. It is beyond words to express my gratitude for the enormous amount of revelation knowledge He has brought into my spirit through His word by the Holy Spirit. And I am beyond excited for all that He still has yet to reveal. I could not imagine life on this earth without Him. I would hate to see even a glimpse of what my life would have been like without Him. I am grateful for the anointing that He placed upon me to write this book. I am not a writer by profession, and there is no way I could have done it without Him.

I would like to thank my family and especially my wife for their patience and support through this endeavor. I could not even begin to count the minutes, hours, days, and months I have spent behind this keyboard.

I would like to thank everyone at Trilogy Publishing. Every department was very supportive and easy to work with.

Also, I would like to thank James Tayor, a friend and a brother in the lord who helped in the beginning to get this book project started.

TABLE OF CONTENTS

Acknowledgments 3
Introduction 7

Chapter 1: *What Is Life, and Where Did We Get It?* 9
Chapter 2: *The Meaning of Life* 29
Chapter 3: *Who Are We?* 35
Chapter 4: *The Five Simple Truths* 43
Chapter 5: *The Five Simple Truths—First… Faith* 47
Chapter 6: *The Five Simple Truths—Second… Jesus* 65
Chapter 7: *The Five Simple Truths—Third… Seed Time and Harvest* 85
Chapter 8: *The Five Simple Truths—Fourth… Forgiveness* . 93
Chapter 9: *The Five Simple Truths—Fifth… Love* 101
Chapter 10: *The Devil's Four Greatest Weapons* 109
Chapter 11: *The Devil's Secret Weapon Word* 131
Chapter 12: *The Five-Step Battle Plan* 139
Chapter 13: *Redeemed from the Curse of the Law* 143
Chapter 14: *Faith Destroying Misconceptions* 149
Chapter 15: *How to Be Led by the Spirit* 161
Chapter 16: *Pay It Forward!* 169
Chapter 17: *Executing the Meaning of Life* 175

Seven Steps to an Answered Prayer 189
The Ephesians Prayer for Revelation Knowledge 195
Psalm 91 Prayer 197
Suggested Study Resource Materials 199

References 201
About the Author 203

INTRODUCTION

I believe most Christians feel like I did. As a young Christian forty years ago, I would read God's word and see all the miraculous and wonderful promises God gave us in His word. However, I did not see the manifestation of these promises, be it spiritually, physically, or financially, in my life or even in the church with any consistency. Sure, I would hear a testimony here or there about a healing or a financial breakthrough. Still, what I was seeing in the natural did not line up with God's word and his promises. Most of the time, I felt like I was praying, as if I was playing the lottery or rolling the spiritual dice.

When you pray for an answer to a need in your life, you are hoping that you will be the lucky one and that God will grant your prayer. To be honest, we have all felt this way from time to time. This may be a lot of Christians' reality, but that is not the way God designed it for us. This set me on a quest thirty-five years ago.

Since then, I have devoured God's word, read hundreds of books, listened to thousands of sermons, and graduated from Rhema Bible College. In this quest through revelation knowledge, God has shown me the simplicity of the full gospel of Jesus Christ and how to apply it in everyday life. As a child of God based on God's word and His promises, we should see and experience victory and miracles on a regular basis. Miracles are nothing more than God's word and His promises coming to pass in the physical realm.

In this book, one will learn how ridiculously simple it is to operate in the Kingdom of God with power, authority, and success. Operating in the Kingdom of God through **faith** is actually very simple; man has made it complicated. In God's word, He said, *"you will know the truth, and the truth will set you free"* (John 8:32 NIV). If you are being set free, what are you getting set free from?

The devil's only weapon is deception, and once the deceptive scales fall from your eyes, you will be set free to see how simple it is to live in the miraculous that God has planned for your life. Each chapter will be a fundamental step to a place where you learn how ridiculously simple it is… the way God designed it to be.

Everything that I had learned over the years was tested by the devil (not God). On December 17th, 2019, my son died at Keck Hospital in Los Angeles, CA, and was dead for forty-three minutes. By implementing what I learned and what is discussed in this book, God raised him from the dead. Hallelujah, glory to God! You, too, will learn that you have the raising from the dead power living inside of you as well!

CHAPTER 1

What Is Life, and Where Did We Get It?

In order to walk in power and fulfill the meaning of our life as God truly intends, we will need to learn how to operate in the supernatural spiritual realm through **faith**. Where miracles exist and are available to us as a child of God. 1 John 4:17 (KJV) says, "as he [Jesus] is, so are we in this world. Miracles are nothing more than God's word and His promises coming to pass in the natural realm. We should see miracles on a regular basis. However, in order to do that, we must learn how to renew our minds so we can apply God's word correctly.

The spirit that lives inside of you (where God inhabits) is more powerful than you could ever dream or imagine. However, it is useless to you until you learn who you truly are in Christ in order to operate in the Kingdom of God.

The goal of this book is to help you learn to unleash what is inside of you as God intended. We will cover all aspects of our three-part being so that you will understand that they are all in harmony with each other to achieve the miraculous God has planned for your life. It is a package deal, and we will get to all of it later. However, first, we need to lay the foundation.

Each chapter will be a foundational step to lead you to a place where you learn how ridiculously simple it is to operate in the Kingdom of God in the supernatural spiritual realm. However, we need to kill some sacred cows and build the correct biblical foundation first to get there. This book is based on the full gospel of Jesus Christ and what I have learned from God's word through revelation knowledge by the Holy Spirit, mentors, and life experiences, as well as observing it in others.

The average Christian today only operates in a small fraction of the full gospel of Jesus Christ, but that is about to change. Jesus died and paid for us to have a five-course meal at a 5-star restaurant. And yet, most Christians spend their whole life eating crumbs off the floor, even though the tab had already been paid in full on our behalf. Operating in the Kingdom of God is way easier than you think. Man has made it complicated.

I will convey what I learned in a condensed version of the most important objectives and how to apply God's word correctly in our everyday lives. My goal was to keep this book short but impactful so that it would be user-friendly and easy to recall and apply for the inevitable attacks of the enemy. And more importantly, my goal is to avoid them in the first place. It will kind of be like getting a letter from your future self to avoid some of the pitfalls and wrong thinking that keep you from living in the miraculous. Also, I want to convey how I would describe the meaning of life and how to achieve it.

First, you would have to define the phrase *"the meaning of life."* And to do that, you would have to define the word **life** itself. The one thing we all know for sure is that we have life. I promise you that if you are reading this book, you have life. So, where did our life come from, and how did we receive it?

The life that we have inside of us came from the very spirit of God Himself. Once God creates a life from Himself, it can never die, just like Him. The life that God gives you is an eternal spirit that will live for eternity. However, the how and where our spirit lives for eternity is up to us. As a child of God, His life lives in us.

> *That they all may be one, as You, Father, are in Me, and I in You; that they also may be one in Us, that the world may believe that You sent Me. And the glory which You gave Me I have given them, that they may be one just as We are one: I in them, and You in Me; that they may be made perfect in one, and that the world may know that You have sent Me, and have loved them as You have loved Me.*
>
> — John 17:21–23 (NJKV)

Jesus prayed that we would be as one with them as they were with each other. If you think about it and spend some time meditating on it, it will blow your mind. The life of God created the world with just a word out of His mouth, and this whole universe fits in His hand, and He lives and operates inside of you. You have the same power in you that parted the Red Sea and raised Jesus from the dead. Jesus Himself now lives inside of you by the Holy Spirit.

If you could truly receive revelation knowledge of who you are in Christ, your abilities are endless because His abilities are endless. Hallelujah, glory to God! This speaks volumes about who you are and what you are capable of on this earth. It does not matter what the world's view of you is or even your view of yourself, but what matters is how God sees you. You are God's pride and joy! He specially designed and created your life out of His life from within Himself for a particular destiny. Further, our most important basic God-given built-in human instinct is to protect that life while we are on this earth and to achieve the meaning of life He planned for us.

In order to pursue the meaning of life, we first have to protect that life that God gave us. Likewise, we have to protect our **faith** in and on God's word to be able to achieve the meaning of our lives as well. God said we have an adversary that has come to *"steal and kill and destroy"* (John 10:10 NIV).

So, let me say this right up front because it is the most important thing I will have to say in this book. In fact, this whole book is centered around this statement and agenda. In fact, we will be driving this point home more than once before we are done! So, we must start here with this vital truth…

> *You cannot wait for the enemy to show up at your gate and think you have time to prepare for a battle.*
> *If you are not prepared in advance…*
> *If you have not built your* fortified wall of protection…
> *If you have not built up your military, arsenal, and strength and are not prepared for battle by renewing your mind with the word of God before the enemy shows up…*
> *You have lost the war before it even began.*

Equally important is the fact that not as many enemies will come to your gate to start with if you do these things. As the old saying goes, "Project strength to avoid conflict."[1]

> *What will happen in the future when the enemy comes for you, your health, children, financial resources, joy, peace, and destiny?*
>
> *Will you have been fortified, trained, and prepared for battle?*
>
> *Will you have a renewed mind?*
>
> *There is no escaping it. We will all face battles on this earth.*
>
> *The devil is the antichrist, and you are Christ's, so we have an enemy.*
>
> *Be sober, be vigilant; because your adversary the devil walks about like a roaring lion, seeking whom he may devour.*
>
> — 1 Peter 5:8 (NKJV)

He has come to kill, steal, and destroy.

> *The thief does not come except to steal, and to kill, and to destroy. I have come that they may have life, and that they may have it more abundantly.*
>
> — John 10:10 (NKJV)

---

[1] Bohdi Sanders, "Project Strength to Avoid Conflict ~ Bohdi Sanders," *The Wisdom Warrior* (blog), February 17, 2016, https://thewisdomwarrior.com/2016/02/17/project-strength-to-avoid-conflict/.

However, if we are prepared, we can devour him instead. Jesus came and paid the price at the cross so that we may have life and life more abundantly. Can we have an abundant life if we are sick, broke, and depressed? More on this area later.

Now, let's get back to the subject of the life that lives within us. Moses was allowed to see out of his peripheral vision with God putting his hand over Mose's eyes. This shielded him and only allowed him to see the reflection of the backside of God. The life of God was still so powerful that it impacted Moses so strongly that his face glowed for a long time just from the effect of it. The children of Israel were so afraid of the glow that Moses had to put a veil over his face. It impacted Moses' physical body almost more than he could withstand. Unlike you and I today, our spirit has been born again by the redemption of the cross; Moses's body could not handle the life of God as a child of God can today with a newly born spirit.

On the mount of configuration, Peter, James, and John were given the opportunity to see the life that lived inside of Jesus. It was so powerful and brilliant that they fell to the earth on their faces. The soldiers in the garden of Gethsemane received a dose of it and fell to the ground like dead men. Jesus explained to the Samaritan woman at the well that it was a perpetual life-giving water that would never dry up, and she would never be thirsty again.

So, when you have revelation knowledge and understand that the life of Christ now lives in you, and you will begin to comprehend who you are in Christ. It truly will just blow your mind! The life that now lives within you is capable of taking hell by storm. In the name of Jesus, you can heal the sick, raise the dead, open the eyes of the blind, and take complete authority over the devil and the kingdom of darkness. Not because of anything we have done but because of what Jesus paid for on our behalf at the cross. Because of the life of God that now lives within us as a child of God. More on this in a later chapter, but just know that you have life, and the life that you have comes from the Father.

However, in order to live this life God gave us and fulfill the meaning of our lives, we must first renew our minds. So, we think like God does and how He wants us to think. What does it mean to be transformed by the renewing of your mind? What does **renewing of the mind** mean in the Bible? "Simply stated, renewing your mind according to Romans 12:2 means interpreting life through the lens of God's word" with revelation knowledge received by "the inspiration of the Holy Spirit."[2] Rather than viewing the natural realm through the lens of your flesh—experience, woundedness, trauma, preferences, bias, old mindsets, or the opinions of others. Romans 12:2 (KJV) states that we are transformed by the renewing of the mind,

> *And be not conformed to this world: but be ye transformed by the renewing of your mind, that ye may prove what is that good, and acceptable, and perfect, will of God.*

In other words, stop thinking and operating in your flesh, being conformed to this world and limited by our five

---

2   Rik, "What Does the Bible Say about Changes in Your Life?," *Self Growth Resources* (blog), November 2, 2022, https://selfgrowthresources.com/what-does-the-bible-say-about-changes-in-your-life/.

physical senses. We transform our minds by God's word and His promises, which is His perfect will. You are renewing your mind to become the **mind of Christ**. Also, when you obtain the mind of Christ, you start thinking like Him, believing like Him, and you start operating with His authority and acting like Him. Once your mind is renewed with the truth in God's word of who you are in Christ, your life will become **transformed**.

We have to renew our minds on how to start thinking and believing in the spiritual realm, on God's word, and His promises. Again, we need to stop being dominated in the flesh by the devil in the natural and emotional realm. Once our minds are renewed, we will no longer think through the flesh and be limited by the five physical senses in the natural realm. Then, we will start thinking like God and operating in the supernatural spiritual realm. In other words, we are not bound or limited to what can be seen through our five physical senses in the natural realm. We are operating in the supernatural spiritual realm by **faith**. We are standing on God's word and His promises that exist in the supernatural realm. We are pulling these promises from God's word into existence in the natural realm. You are operating in the Kingdom of God in the supernatural realm through and by **faith**. Faith will be discussed in a later chapter. For now, let's stay on the topic of renewing our minds.

If you have not figured it out by now, I am and will be driving this point home repeatedly and overwhelmingly. I am passionate about getting this so deeply embedded in your spirit until it becomes a hunger and a quest burning in your soul. Everything we endeavor hinges on our openness, drive, and ability to have our minds renewed. This hunger and drive from revelation knowledge about wanting and needing our minds renewed is the ship that God has for us, which has already been given and paid for, and we are going to be sailing on.

You must want it so badly that it will motivate you to get your lazy self off the couch and chase after it like a dog after a bone... LOL. Please, oh please, you have to get this. Because if you cannot (a) understand that you must renew your mind, (b) why the importance of renewing your mind, or (C) how to renew your mind, you cannot be transformed. Plus, if you cannot be transformed, you will never be able to accomplish all the things in this book, understand what is being discussed in this book, or anything that God wants you to accomplish in your life. Receiving revelation knowledge about the need for renewing your mind is the spark that lights the flame of hunger so your life can be transformed. Transformed from rags to riches, as they say.

You are transformed by operating in the spirit, in the supernatural spiritual realm through **faith**, instead of being limited in the flesh by just your five physical senses. Also, you must renew your mind with the truth in both realms. You cannot operate effectively in truth in the supernatural spiritual realm while holding on to lies in your soul (mind, flesh) in the natural realm. When you renew your mind on God's word, the Holy Spirit leads you to the truth in both realms. This is the **mind of Christ** versus the **mindset** you receive in the natural that is based on lies, deception, propaganda, demographics, geographics, social media, your buddy down the street, or just whomever or whatever had most of your attention at the time.

The devil attacks us in our minds, especially in our emotions, because our minds are the battlefield. As children of God begin to build revelation knowledge through the word of God and learn about God's word and His promises, our minds are renewed. "What you feed your mind with becomes a mindset. A mindset is impossible to change without changing what your mind is filled with."[3]

Typically, when we hear the truth about a subject, we try to change our mindset. However, everyone who knows us quickly learns that it is impossible without **total** renewal of our minds. This past mindset has control of us, and it rejects and deflects truth from our controlled narrative so fast that our souls never have a chance even to get wind of it if we are truly honest with ourselves. Because a mindset controls us whether we realize it or not, and whether we like it or not. Most of the time, we are controlled by this mindset, and we do not even recognize it. We are thinking through a lens of bias that has become so deeply rooted that we do not know it exists or how it even got there. In the process, the devil has us brainwashed and blind to the truth. Truth is in both realms: truth in the spiritual realm and truth in the natural realm.

We spend years building this mindset and are completely oblivious to everything that transpired to even give us that mindset. It started in childhood. The devil's only weapon against us is deception. How did we receive this enormous false and biased mindset? We received this mindset from all the lies we have swallowed from the enemy. We gained this enormous false and biased mindset. It is like how you would eat an elephant... one bite (lie) at a time.

---

[3] Vladimir Savchuk, "7 Steps to Renew Your Mind," Vladimir Savchuk Ministries, January 17, 2021, https://pastorvlad.org/mindrenewal/.

The only way to change your default and automatic past mind set is to…

1. be open to the possibility that this past biased mindset was built upon lies, could still exist, and it will keep you from the truth.
2. renew your mind with truth.

What Truth? The truth of God's word and His promises, as well as the truth that exists in the natural realm. There is no such thing as **my truth**. That is fantasy land. Either something is true, or it is false. It is either God's truth or the devil's lies. Also, that is true in the spiritual realm and just as equally in the natural realm. So, you need to learn the truth of who you are in Christ and all He has done for you. Then, you need to learn what is true in the natural realm by being led by the Holy Spirit. In the upcoming chapters, topics such as the *Five Simple Truths* and what to renew our minds with will be discussed.

Our minds are the battlefield where we are in warfare with the devil. However, the devil will never attack a born-again child of God in the spiritual realm. Our spirit is perfect, our **faith** is perfect, it is engulfed with the Holy Spirit, the life of God lives within it, and we are robed in the righteousness of Christ. He does not stand a chance with that package in the spiritual realm. Our spirit and **faith** are perfect and ten feet tall and bulletproof. It is our minds (souls) that are vulnerable.

The devil will only come at you in the physical realm through your soul, in your mind, will, and emotions. He will try to keep you from learning who you are in Christ and all that He has done for you. More importantly, the devil will work double overtime to steal any truth that may have come across your path in God's garden of revelation knowledge. Again, the only weapon the devil has against you is deception. Because once you renew your mind with revelation knowledge from the word of God of who you are in Christ, it becomes your new mindset. Then, the devil cannot stand against you in any realm.

This is when you become dangerous to the kingdom of darkness, powerful and productive for the Kingdom of God… living a successful Christian life so that you can experience the meaning of your life. So, renewing your mind is just feeding on God's word as much as possible. A renewed mind is based on God's word and His promises by the full gospel of Jesus Christ and not a watered-down religion that will leave you powerless, and to renew your mind slowly by replacing your old mindset and the lies that were created with the word of God. Then, be led to truth by the Holy Spirit for all the truth in the natural realm.

When we are renewing our minds, we must take the mindset that God's word gets first place in every and all situations. And when I say God's word gets first place over everything, I mean **everything**. In order to do this, we must learn how to suspend natural human, fleshly thinking *"conformed to this world"* (Romans 12:2 NKJV). That is based on the physical realm and the laws that govern it.

Miracles do not exist in the natural realm. They can only come from the spiritual realm. However, you are a spirit being operating in the spiritual realm through **faith** that supersedes the natural realm. You are no longer bound by physical law. It is said in the verse above, *"do not be conformed to this world."* You are operating in the spiritual realm, in the Kingdom of God that supersedes the five physical senses.

Now, with our renewed minds, we are **transformed** to be able to operate in the supernatural spiritual realm with the **mind of Christ** through our **faith** that is based on God's word and His promises. It is not based on the devil's deception or a watered-down religion that may have been indoctrinated within us. The supernatural spiritual gift that gives us the ability to operate in the supernatural spiritual realm is **faith**.

So, once your mind is renewed, it starts being transformed to think and operate in the spiritual realm, where you are no longer bound by the five physical senses. In order to operate in faith, you can no longer be controlled or ruled by your five physical senses. In fact, if you can see it with your five physical senses, then it is not **faith**. (More on this later.)

Each one of us was given *"the measure of faith"* (Romans 12:3 KJV). It is a gift from God by grace at salvation, and every believer has the same amount of faith. We have been given *"the measure of faith."* Faith is a gift that allows us to operate in the spiritual realm. What we do with that gift of **faith** is up to us, not God.

Another definition of faith is the **absence of unbelief**. I had better stop there before I get too excited and start writing out of a different chapter; we will get to all of this later. However, the point to remember at this time is to understand that while reading this book, you are starting the process of renewing your mind. From this point forward, whether you are reading God's word, this book, or anything else that would help you gain knowledge of the word of God, you are renewing your mind. For example, Mark 11:23 says that we can *speak to* *mountains* and have them removed. This is a parable, and the mountains that we are supposed to speak to are the mountains that the devil puts before us to destroy us.

Renewing our minds is not adapting to a watered-down religion that gives us some excuse for why we are not operating in this verse like God said we could and should. Watered-down religion says (prays) things like "If it be God's will."

Renewing your mind is studying God's word to learn...

1. What God's will is.
2. Why it is not operating in your life so that you can begin learning how to do it.
3. To not only do what God said you could do but to be even stronger because He commissioned you to do it.

Part of renewing our minds is learning that we have the authority in the name of Jesus to speak to these mountains directly. Consciously, we should be thinking that we are indeed renewing our minds. We have to remove these old, biased mindsets and replace them with our new mindset, **the mind of Christ**. So, we constantly need to keep in the back of our minds that we are purposely changing our old mindset by constantly renewing our minds with truth from God's word. When we think about it, it becomes a goal and an objective to renew our minds.

Remember, have fun along the way and enjoy the awesome feeling when the Holy Spirit shows you something personally out of God's word. That is direct revelation knowledge from the Holy Spirit that renews your mind that the devil could not steal from you if his life depended upon it. We renew our minds by meditating on God's word and His promises, which will renew our minds and build our new mindset with God's word and His promises.

The definition of meditate:

> *"Think deeply or focus one's mind for a period of time, in silence or with the aid of chanting, repeating and reciting in your mind truths, for religious or spiritual purposes. or as a method of relaxation think deeply or carefully about something."*[4]

So, when you are meditating on God's word, you are repeating it over and over again in your mind, every aspect of the word you were given in your heart by the Holy Spirit. Let me give you an example. Let's say that you received revelation knowledge about this verse:

> *I can do all things through Christ which strengthens me.*
>
> — Philippians 4:13 (NKJV)

Then, you meditate on this verse, and you start thinking and speaking things in and under your breath in your mind like this…

---

[4] "Meditate," The Oxford Pocket Dictionary of Current English. Encyclopedia.com., accessed June 17, 2024, https://www.encyclopedia.com/humanities/dictionaries-thesauruses-pictures-and-press-releases/meditate-0.

I can pay my bills through Christ, which strengthens me.

I can receive my healing through Christ, which strengthens me.

I can receive that promotion or raise through Christ, which strengthened me etc.

This is meditating on God's word, not just reading it like a book.

> *This book of the law shall not depart out of thy mouth; but thou shalt meditate therein day and night, that thou mayest observe to do according to all that is written therein: for then thou shalt make thy way prosperous, and then thou shalt have good success.*
>
> — Joshua 1:8 (KJV)

By meditating on God's word, look who makes *"thy way prosperous?"* Remember, Moses just died, and Joshua is picking up his mantle and leadership over all the children and tribes of Israel at this moment. Can you imagine the overwhelming stress of replacing Moses? The man who walked around with his face glowing from the life of God and parting the Red Sea. Believe me, the world was on his shoulders.

However, look who God told him would make his way prosperous and how? *"For then thou shalt make thy way prosperous,"* and then thou shalt have good success" (Joshua 1:8 KJV)."

Who makes their way prosperous? *"Thou shalt,"* which means you do! And how do you do it? By *meditating on his word day and night,* renewing your mind with God's word and His promises. This is not based on anything that you did but based on what Jesus did.

You start renewing your mind to have a new mindset, which is the **mind of Christ**. Then you start walking in the authority of everything that Christ paid for you! You start devouring God's word, this book, or anything you can get your hands on to renew your mind. Then, keep reading it over and over until it gets embedded in your mind and spirit. You keep meditating on everything the Holy Spirit puts in your spirit until you find out who you are in Christ by knowing all that He has paid for you on the cross. By doing this, you start walking in a whole new level of purpose, power, and success than you could have ever imagined.

Think of your old, biased mindset as a bucket filled to the rim, full of lies and deception. Renewing your mind is not instantly removing all the lies from the bucket, which is almost impossible to do. Remember, old mindsets do not die easily because it took years to build them. It is ever-increasingly adding truth to the bucket until the truth displaces all the lies, deception, and unbelief that the devil filled it with and has deceived you… us. However, when you have a new bucket full of truth, your mind is renewed, and you have a new mindset, the **mind of Christ** in **Spirit and truth**!

Renewing your mind is finding out all that has been purchased for you at the cross. All the awesome things Jesus purchased for you on the cross have no value to you if you do not have revelation knowledge of what has been given to you and how to apply them. It all belongs to you, but if you do not know it, it will not do you any good. Renewing your mind is finding out in God's word all that Jesus purchased for you at the cross.

You could have a diamond mine in your backyard, but if you do not know about it, you would be a broke billionaire struggling to pay the bills. That is the main deception of the devil. His most important objective is to keep you from finding out who you truly are in Christ and the power and authority that lives within you. Because once you do, and his deceptive scales have been removed from your eyes by renewing your mind, he is absolutely powerless against you. That mountain will absolutely crumble before you in the name of Jesus. It has to; it is God's spiritual law!

God's spiritual law is more real than the law of gravity in the natural realm. It is backed up by God's word if you speak God's word by faith, which He said,

> *So shall my word be that goeth forth out of my mouth: it shall not return unto me void, but it shall accomplish that which I please, and it shall prosper in the thing whereto I sent.*
>
> —Isaiah 55:11 (KJV)

Who is the liar here? God's word that says you can, or watered-down religions that say you cannot? It says in God's word, Romans 3:4 (NKJV), *"let God be true, but every man a liar."* All of the lies the devil has used to deceive you will be eliminated when you renew your mind. Deception is the devil's only weapon against you. Renewing your mind is being set free from all his deception and lies.

When you renew your mind with God's word as well as the things that are covered in this book, you can start living in complete victory in every area of your life. When you have a renewed mind, you start taking the limits off of God's word and His promises and start walking in confidence, knowing who you are in Christ. You will no longer be bound to the natural realm with your five physical senses. You then will be operating in the spiritual realm where miracles exist and bring them into the natural realm by **faith**.

In God's word, it says, *"And ye shall know the truth, and the truth shall make [set] you free"* (John 8:32 KJV). When renewing your mind with God's word, you are getting set free. So, if you are getting set free, what are you getting set free from? You are getting set free from all the lies the devil and this world has put on and in you—all the lies in both realms. Lies to keep you from knowing who you are in Christ. Lies to keep you from walking in victory. Lies to keep you from fulfilling God's plan for your life. Lies to keep you from walking in perfect health. Lies to keep you from receiving your healing. Lies to keep you from walking in prosperity. Lies to keep you from walking in peace, joy, and authority. Lies to keep you from being an effective weapon for the Kingdom of God, yourself, and others around you.

I could keep going because the devil's lies are endless. But praise the Lord; God's word and truth are even more endless. I did my best to explain what renewing your mind is, how important it is, and how to do it. Please let me strongly encourage you to start renewing your mind today. It is the beginning of a new life that is far beyond your wildest dreams and prayers. In the following chapters, you will start to discover what to use to renew your mind.

CHAPTER 2
The Meaning of Life

Most would write a point of view on a subject and finish with a summary that puts everything discussed into perspective. I am going to do this in reverse. And start out with a direct, bold, and unfiltered statement about the meaning of life and then explain it thereafter. For the shock factor or just calling a spade a spade, as they say, or to see the narrative and objective in advance.

It is absolutely ludicrous and foolish to think anyone could live their life on their own, following their desires, trusting in their strength while trying to pursue what they think will make them happy and finish out their life here on earth with the feeling of contentment, satisfaction, joy, peace, and success. Or should we live a life with purpose without an intimate relationship with our creator, who put us on this earth for a purpose? Without pursuing the life we were purposed for, we will never experience anything other than dead-end roads full of disappointments and will never achieve a feeling of true happiness and contentment or accomplishment… Or at least not anything that lasts but for a small fraction of time.

Everything we try to do in the process will just leave us empty, and we will never really attain true happiness. To try to achieve anything without God and His plan and purpose for our lives on our strength, on our plan, will constantly leave us with a feeling of incompetence, fear, anxiety, and that constant fear of being a failure, including failure itself in all areas of our lives. If we do not build up our spiritual armor in advance for the inevitable attacks from the enemy, as well as not renewing our minds, we will not be protected from all the evil the devil would like to send into our lives.

Ok, so there it is, but it took half a paragraph to say it to see the true magnitude of it. So, we have to understand that the meaning of life is based on the meaning of our lives, not someone else's. I do not care how many self-proclaimed idiots and philosophers who think they have a cookie-cutter thesis on the subject. In order to achieve the meaning of our lives, we have to follow the life that God established and purposed us for personally. This is not based on the world's view of it but on our own purpose here. That is why no one can judge another person's life. So, the true meaning of life is the one God destined for us to have personally. This is a personal meaning of life; therefore, it can only be defined for you through a walk with God as He leads you day by day into your personal destiny.

Also, think about all the things you do on a daily basis to try to keep yourself occupied with things that are not really all that important, but you elevate them as being such. You mentally put unimportant or trivial everyday tasks ahead of important things. That keeps your mind distracted and busy from facing and doing the really important things that you need to do in your life.

There are many things we do need to do, like mowing the grass, washing clothes, cleaning the house, etc. Unfortunately, we waste so much of our time on meaningless, trivial things when we should have been doing the important things. Then, we justified how important these things are. However, the grass is now a foot high, the dishes are piled up, and we do not have any clean clothes to wear. Then we are forced to do the most important things now. When all along, we should have been doing the things we are responsible for first.

So, what I am saying is… just take 1% of that wasted time and focus on your relationship with God. Time to renew your mind and grow spiritually while you are pursuing God's will for your life. That is the meaning of life… Doing something positive about your future, building your fortified wall and hedge of protection around your life and family by feeding on God's word of who you are in Christ. This can be done through reading a book or researching something you would like to learn to grow your knowledge, etc.

I am not saying we should not have lazy time, having time to just relax and do meaningless things. Lazy time is important, as well as having a balanced life. I surely do plenty of this myself and struggle with doing too much of it, just like everyone else does at times. However, I will say I have slowly built a kind of inner meter within that lets me know when I am taking it too far. Then my conscience slaps me in the face, so to speak.

I liked something that I heard Dr. Jordan B. Peterson say in a podcast that really stuck with me. I cannot remember the exact show, and I am not sure I am wording it like he quoted it. However, this is how I comprehended it. He said, "If you would get up in the morning and sit on the edge of your bed and ask yourself one thing in your life that is holding you back, you will surprisingly get a response instantly from within (your spirit)." Remember, it only takes a few minutes in the morning just to hang out with the Holy Spirit. You just need to spend a little time in His word, renewing your mind, and asking Him what He has planned for your life for that day. There is no definition of the meaning of life other than the one that God destined for you to have personally. Now, I will try to convey why this apophysis is more real and true than you may know and the ways to achieve it.

Let me start off by asking you to ask yourself a question. Think about something from your past that you thought if you could only have a particular something or achieve something, you would be the happiest person on earth. Now, ask yourself how much value and contentment does it have in your life right now, today, at this moment? I am not saying if we try hard enough, we cannot find some things that would fit that category because God gives us our strengths and abilities to achieve certain things in life. Thus, by just having a built-in interest given to us by God to equip us for our destiny, we can accidentally levitate to a fraction of what God has planned for us. However, for most things, we become bored with them pretty quickly, and then they are not so fulfilling anymore and no longer have much value. We are then back to being as empty as we were to start with—still looking for something that will bring us happiness and contentment. What kind of life is that? How would you ever live a meaningful, satisfying life like that?

Now, imagine doing this for the rest of your life. Going after something, obtaining it (or not), getting bored, feeling empty, then repeating, repeating, repeating. And even worse than that, spending your whole life going after the things you never had the ability to achieve because that was not your intended destiny. As they say, to keep doing the same thing and expect to get different results is ludicrous. How do I know this? Because I have done this too much and watched so many people around me do it as well. However, God slowly started showing me things, and I realized you can never achieve or attain enough to fill that void. Only God and His purpose for your life can achieve it. To this day, my most consistent prayer is asking Him to help me to stay in His will as He guides me.

Also, remember that walking out God's will for your life is a day-by-day adventure. Also, it does not take any time out of your life to put something on your phone beside your bed at night when you are going to sleep to listen to and build yourself up spiritually.

So, it really does not take a lot of time or effort to better your life, especially considering it's the most important thing you will have done that day. It is just a matter of comprehending the importance of it and giving it the priority it deserves. Just remember to schedule a little time accordingly, considering the importance of it. While you are doing this, you are simultaneously building your fortified wall of protection over your life by feeding on God's word and His promises of who you are in Christ.

CHAPTER 3

Who Are We?

Now, let's look at who we are and how God created us. We are a three-part being: body, soul, and spirit. In reality, who we are is a spirit that will live for eternity. And that is forever. The only reason we have the other two parts is to be able to operate on this earth for a short period of time. This allows us to be able to operate on this earth temporarily to fulfill our destiny here as well as be trained for eternity. He put in us our strengths, desires, and weaknesses to help us navigate His will for our lives, which is the meaning of life.

God had a plan and purpose for our life before He ever put us in our mother's womb. We are here to be trained not just for our purpose here on this earth but also God has a plan for us for eternity. So, if we are not following God's plan, we could spend our whole time on this earth trying to fulfill the desires of our body and soul and never reach our destiny or purpose.

For instance, if God built you to be a socket wrench and you think that by being a screwdriver you will be happy, you are deceived by your adversary and will be a failure in life even if you had a billion dollars in the bank during the process. Because if your purpose in life was to remove a bolt, you would spend your whole life trying to get that bolt out with your screwdriver, and you would never succeed and never be satisfied. Because that is not what your intended purpose is. You would always be living in a place of failure, fear, incompetence, low self-esteem, and emptiness, trying to achieve something you were never designed or created to do. Even if you did end up in life with that big bank account by chance, think of your spirit as the parent and your body and soul (mind) as little children. The spirit knows what's best for the children, but all children care about is me, me, me, me. They are always desiring something new, and no matter what you give them, they just keep wanting something different and more, more, and more. Still, nothing you will ever give them will completely satisfy them for any length of time.

> *But you have an anointing from the Holy One, and you know all things.*
>
> — 1 John 2:20 (NKJV)

In true reality, your spirit is the real you, and your body (flesh) is nothing more than a temporary rental car. And yet most people have it in reverse and just try to focus on the flesh, but their spirit, which is the very one that is supposed to be in control, is locked up and down in the basement. Therefore, they never will experience a life of true fulfillment, satisfaction, containment, happiness, peace, or accomplishment. Nor will they ever walk in power and authority on this earth as God intended for them.

God has a personalized plan for your life and destiny, and you can try to fulfill it with everything on this earth, from relationships, careers, activities, material things, sex, drugs, and rock'n'roll… LOL. However, you will never achieve the happiness and euphoria that you will have when you follow

God's particular plan for your life—through having a personal, intimate relationship with Him. That is why I think drugs and alcohol have the strongest pull on people because it is a satanic copycat of what it is like to be high in the spirit realm. Instead, we should be high on the contentment we receive when we follow God's plan for our lives, which we cannot receive through anything else. When we fall for the deceptive copycat, not the genuine article, that the devil is pushing on us, it keeps us from our true calling and our heart's desires for our whole lives.

I think the higher the draw of these things on certain people indicatives a higher calling God has on that individual's life. The devil is the antichrist; the word **Christ** means anointed. So, in essence, the devil is anti-anointing because he is afraid of people who are anointed to achieve great things for God, other people, and themselves on this earth. Therefore, his only defense against an anointed life is to defeat us by deception with these copycats and lies to try to deceive, distract, and destroy us.

Making time on a daily basis to fellowship with God and His word is more important than what church we attend to renew our minds and build our biblical foundation. I am not saying we should not go to church; we 100% should. However, if we went to church every time the doors opened, it would only be three times a week. Most people just go on Sunday morning or not at all. So, it is our personal time of fellowship, meditation, prayer, and Bible study that is the real contributing factor to renewing our minds to succeed on this earth. This is a time to hang out with the Holy Spirit and talk to Him, building our relationship with Him. It is a time to renew our minds by feeding on God's words and His promises. In the process, we are building our revelation knowledge of who we are in Christ. Also, ask Him where He is leading us to our next adventure—navigating us through every turn in our life, one crossroad at a time.

Now, I would like to expand upon our three-part being. We are made of three components: body, soul, and spirit. With our bodies, we make contact and operate in the physical realm. With our souls (minds), we make contact and operate in the natural/intellectual realm. And with our spirits, we make contact and operate in the spirit, in the spiritual realm. Our spirit is who we truly are, and the other two components are nothing more than tools to use for the purpose of achieving God's destiny for our lives here on this earth to take us into eternity. Let's dive into each one of these realms separately to get a true analytical perspective.

How much time and effort do we focus on our body, its nutritional and physical needs, and its selfish wants, desires, and addictions on a daily basis? From eating, sanitizing, beautification, maintenance, and recreation, good and bad, etc. What would happen to our bodies if we ignored them, put things in them that were not good for them, and only gave them a little snack once a week at best or nothing at all? Would it become weak, frail, ugly, non-useful, or even die?

What about our minds (souls)? What if we never used them or gave them any intellectual nourishment or engagement? Would our minds not become unproductive, uninformed, and stupid? So, how could anyone expect us to become fulfilled, strong, and powerful spiritually if we only gave our spirits one small snack a week at best or nothing at all? Would it also become weak, frail, stupid, and unproductive?

What is important to understand is that out of our three components, the body, soul, and spirit, our spirits are actually the most important thing we possess; it is the real us and who we are, along with our souls (minds). Because we only take these two into eternity! Our spirits are our life because that is where the Holy Spirit inhabits. It is not the remaining two that consume the bulk of our precious time. And yet, you pull a spirit out of the body, and it will drop like a bag of rocks with no life in it.

Your spirit is your life. Unfortunately, most people spend their time in the physical realm concerning their bodies, and this is the only one of the three that we only use for a short period of time. Then we cast it away, back to the dirt from which it came. This is why most Christians have a hard time operating in the supernatural spirit realm. This is because they spend the majority of their time in the physical realm. At the age of 62, my life that is behind me, now only seems like a blink of an eye. So, to spend most of our priority on the shortest term and the disposable part of us is ludicrous. Does this make sense?

With that said, I am not trying to put anyone in condemnation over this because we all struggle with it. God took on flesh (through Jesus) and came to this earth, and He understands our humanity. Still, we need to be mindful of the reality of this and its importance to keep it in perspective. We should not try to measure ourselves against someone else but measure ourselves personally. The measure should be that we have more knowledge about God's word and His promises today than we had yesterday. That is how we grow spiritually, one day at a time.

If we want to operate in the matrix of the Kingdom of God with power, authority, and miracles, we must grow spiritually. It is imperative that we try to set aside time for our spirits just like we do our bodies and souls (minds) on a consistent basis. We should not be narrow-minded about all things temporal while ignoring the most important, which is eternal.

Like I said earlier, when you have a renewed mind operating in the spirit realm, you start taking the limits off of God's word and His promises. Then you start walking in victory and confidence, knowing who you are in Christ and all that He has purchased for you. You will no longer be bound to the natural realm with your five physical senses. You then will be operating in the supernatural realm where miracles exist and bring them into the natural realm by faith. However, in order to do this, we need to build ourselves up spiritually. We need to become more spiritually conscious than physically conscious. We have to realize who we truly are as spirit beings and let our spirits run and control us like God intended our three-part being to function.

You are a spirit being that can and should be operating in the spiritual realm. My question to you is… Do you want to be stuck in the physical realm where miracles do not exist and are limited, dominated, and controlled by your five physical senses? Then just keep doing what you are doing, live in this physical realm, and focus all your time on your physical body with your unrenewed mind. However, if you want to operate on this earth as God intended, you have to build yourself up spiritually by renewing your mind and letting your spirit control and guide your three-part being.

> *Wherefore lay apart all filthiness and superfluity of naughtiness, and receive with meekness the engrafted word, which is able to save your souls.*
>
> — James 1:21 (KJV)

While reading this verse, keep in mind that James is writing to a Christian Church congregation. This letter was not written to non-believers. He is telling them (Christians) to use the engrafted word of God to *"save their souls"* (mind and flesh).

So, we have to understand that at salvation, our spirits are born again and are saved as well as in union with Christ as one. However, our souls (minds) have to be saved by the renewing of our minds. Again, many people use the words spirit and soul interchangeably, but you cannot do that; they are not the same thing. Our spirits are the real us and are instantly transformed, robed in the righteousness of Christ, and adopted into the Kingdom of God's dear Son. As well as, our spirits are one with Christ Jesus. Therefore, our souls (minds) have to be renewed by the word of God so they can be in line and agree with our spirits, which are now perfect.

Renewing your mind is building yourself up spiritually so that your spirit and soul work in perfect harmony through revelation knowledge from God's word and His promises to operate in the supernatural spiritual realm effectively with authority and power.

CHAPTER 4

The Five Simple Truths

The next subject is our foundation that we work within to live a successful life as a child of God while on this earth. These truths are the beginning of renewing our minds that have been discussed so much already to be able to pursue the meaning of life. I feel it will be quite comforting when you realize just how incredibly simple it really is.

When we think about God, religion, and theology with all of its comprehensive complexity, it can be a little overwhelming, especially in the beginning. Still, the truth of it is that a personal relationship with God is actually really very simple; man has made it complicated. It just boils down to really only five main simple truths:

- Faith
- Jesus
- Seed time and Harvest
- Forgiveness
- Love

All of these are actually very simple. They all work together in unison with each other. If an individual just read these *Five*

Simple Truths alone over and over again until they became embedded in his/her spirit, they would be miles ahead of most Christians in the walk of life in a very short period of time. These *Five Simple Truths* are the building blocks that help you begin to renew your mind with revelation knowledge of who you are in Christ. They build your fortified wall of protection while operating on this earth.

A theologian could take each one of these truths and turn them into books that are three inches thick. For myself, I did just the opposite. I like the KISS program (keep it simple, stupid). It is not as important to have lots of weapons as it is to be very efficient in the important ones.

In the last 30 years, I have studied God's word personally, listened to thousands of sermons, and read hundreds of books. I also graduated from Rhema Correspondence Bible College. After all of this, I learned, and still am, that it really just boils down to these *Five Simple Truths*, and I would like to share them with you. I call them the *Christian Constitution*.

These truths are going to be your weapons of warfare in order to achieve your meaning in life. Everyone wants to see miracles, and they are awesome! In the early days of learning how to walk by faith, I literally lived from miracle to miracle, especially financially concerning my business.

For so many months, month after month on paper as well as the bank account, technically I would be out of business. I would get in my prayer closet and get my scriptures out of God's word and His promises. Then I would pray, stand on His word, and put God's word in first place over what I saw in the natural. Then, some kind of financial miracle would take place, and I would survive for another month.

I gained more practice praying down miracles than learning how to run my business. Then God started showing me that living from miracle to miracle was not His best for me. If I had to live from miracle to miracle, then there was a problem. If I was operating efficiently in the Kingdom of God with God's word and His promises, applying His word correctly with the *Five Simple Truths*, I would not constantly need a miracle. I could live in His blessing and live a consistent, successful life.

In the next chapters, we will be discussing the *Five Simple Truths*. We will take each truth separately to gain comprehensive revelation knowledge from God's word to truly begin the process of renewing our minds. These truths are the main foundation of this book to help simplify the most vital revelation knowledge that we need to receive to live a successful Christian life to fulfill *The Meaning of Life*.

CHAPTER 5

The Five Simple Truths—First... Faith

L et's start off with the Bible's definition of **faith**:

> *Now faith is the substance of things hoped for, the evidence of things not seen.*
> — Hebrews 11:1 (KJV)

Now, let's understand the importance of **faith**.

> *But without faith it is impossible to please him [God].*
> — Hebrews 11:6 (KJV)

Faith is the vehicle (substance) in which everything in the spiritual realm operates in and travels on. Let's take two people from the Old Testament and compare the two and their approach and relationship with God. They were godly men but had different approaches, lives, and outcomes. Let's take Abraham and Job for contrast and comparison.

Abraham is the **father of our faith**, and he is listed in the eleventh chapter of Hebrews as one of the heroes of faith (Job was not). God justified him with only one thing: **faith**.

In the Old Testament, you do not really see the word **faith**. The word that was used then was **trust**, but they mean the same thing. Abraham was not perfect by any means. Most importantly, he trusted God, and it was imputed unto him as righteousness, and God called him His friend. Also, God blessed him beyond measure. Abraham trusted God to the point that when asked to take his family, leave his home and inheritance, and just start out on a journey to the unknown, he obeyed. He was only trusting God, day by day, where He was leading him, and Abraham did so on **faith** alone.

Abraham also trusted God when asked to sacrifice his only son, and he was willing to do it. Because he knew and had faith in God that even if he sacrificed his son, God would bring him back to him somehow. Genesis 22:5 (NIV) says, *"He said to his servants, 'Stay here with the donkey while I and the boy go over there. We will worship and then we will come back to you.'"* He declared what he believed **we** will worship, and then **we** will come back to you. Because he trusted that God had promised him that his seed would be like the sands in the seashore and the stars in the sky that were too numerous to count. Abraham trusted God that whatever He said, He would do, and He was able to and would perform.

In short, Abraham trusted God with all his heart, and he was considered righteous for faith alone. Due to this, he had a close personal relationship with God. God blessed him so enormously that he actually loaned money to kings. Also, his seed was too numerous to count, just like God had promised, and Abraham is the spiritual father of us all. When we accept Christ as our savior, we become the seed of Abraham and heirs according to the promise.

Job, on the other hand, is a different story. It is sad to say, but I would say that Job would be the equivalent to the average child of God today. Job was a good man, a very benevolent man, and God blessed him also. However, unlike Abraham, Job seemingly went through hell on earth for a period of time. To be honest, I used to hate the story of Job and would actually avoid it as much as possible. It seemed like on the surface that God and the devil were wagering bets over him.

The story of Job contradicted everything I had ever come to understand about God's character, and it was very troubling. Except, one day, I was reading it and the Holy Spirit showed me something that knocked me out of my chair, so to speak. He showed me nine words that I had read many times but never truly saw before that day (revelation knowledge), and it changed everything about Job's story. Job said, *"For the thing which I greatly feared is come upon me, and that which I was afraid of is come unto me"* (Job 3:25 KJV). Then it hit me like a ton of lead. Fear and worry are the polar opposites of faith. They cannot be in the same space at the same time. You are either walking in one or the other, you cannot do both at the same time.

Job was a great man and had all the things listed above, but he lacked one thing that Abraham had, which God required and desired the most of anything else, and that was faith. What God wants and desires from us is an intimate relationship with us.

Think about marriage for a minute. There is no relationship or intimacy if there is no trust and faith. Trust (faith) is the catalyst for an intimate relationship, and there is only one way to build your faith, and that is to practice and exercise it just like you would your physical body. The more you practice faith, the better you'll become. There will be failures along the way, but you learn from them and become stronger.

Kenneth E. Hagin said something while I was listening to one of his sermons years ago, I am not sure which sermon, but it helped me enormously through the trial and error phase (and still am) of operating in faith and dealing with the failures along the way. He said, "If you put the word of God into action and it didn't work, it wasn't God's word, you just didn't apply his word correctly." God said His word would not come back void. So, I would just go into prayer and ask the Holy Spirit where I missed it and help me learn from it. That helped me not to blame God for my failures of not applying His word correctly and why He seemingly abandoned me at times, or at least it felt that way to me. And let me look within myself at my failure to appropriate His word correctly. As that old saying goes, which is evidently now a title to a book, *"Fact's Don't Care about Your Feelings."*

If the devil can get us to blame God for our failures, he will conquer and divide to destroy us. We must put God's word in first place in every situation. I like something else Brother Hagin said in one of his many sermons that I have listened to, and it has really stuck with me over the years as well. He said, "I am not moved by what I see, I am not moved by what I feel, I'm only moved by what God's word says about it." That is putting God's word in first place into operation.

This is where you start learning how to suspend your natural, fleshy human thinking. You must give God's word first place and final authority over **everything** that you see or feel in the natural realm. We must learn that the supernatural spiritual realm is way more real than the physical one and that it is not limited to just the physical realm. The supernatural spiritual realm operates and controls both. The world calls it fantasy, but a child of God calls it faith. What the world cannot receive through fantasy (none of us can), a child of God can through faith. Hallelujah, glory to God!

In order to understand **faith**, you have to comprehend that God has already paid for and given you everything. It is not really a matter of having **faith** for something and waiting for God to give it or perform it. It is a matter of renewing your mind, learning through revelation knowledge from God's word, and how to receive what you have already been given. What Jesus already died for on your behalf so you can receive it by grace through (your) faith. God has already paid for and provided everything for you in advance. So, how do we receive salvation?

Jesus does not **give** us salvation; He **gave** us salvation; that is past tense. He has already given you salvation by His death, burial, and resurrection. It is and was paid for in advance. It is an act of our faith and responsibility to just receive what He has already given, what He already paid for.

Every promise in God's word works the same way. It is not a matter of Him giving it; it is a matter of you having faith and revelation knowledge of how to receive what He has already given you. Like our healing when He took stripes on His back when He was crucified. This was prophesied in the Old Testament long before it was paid for on our behalf by Jesus during His crucifixion in the New Testament as was prophesied.

> *Surely he hath borne our griefs, and carried our sorrows: yet we did esteem him stricken, smitten of God, and afflicted. But he was wounded for our transgressions, he was bruised for our iniquities: the chastisement of our peace was upon him; and with his stripes we are healed.*
>
> — Isaiah 53:4–5 (KJV)

Then Peter referenced it in the New Testament, *"Who his own self bare our sins in his own body on the tree, that we, being dead to sins, should live unto righteousness: by whose stripes ye were healed"* (1 Peter 2:24 KJV). That is past tense. God is not **going** to heal you because he already has! It is a matter of us building our faith in God's word and His promises for healing to receive what He has already paid for and provided in advance.

So, if we do not receive healing, it is not God's fault because He has already paid for it in advance on our behalf. We have the grace and the luxury only to receive what He has already given us by faith. This is why renewing our minds with God's word and His promises is so important. If you want to receive your healing, you have to apply God's word correctly concerning healing, or it will not work.

For most of the years, while building my faith, I did not really understand or have revelation knowledge about this until a few years ago. Until then, I was still trying to build my faith to get God to move on my behalf, and I did not comprehend that He had already moved and had already given it. Therefore, it was up to me to have revelation knowledge of His word and **faith** to receive what He had already provided and given.

Again, every promise in God's word works this way. My son died at Keck Hospital in LA in December of 2019. While I was outside my son's hospital room in prayer and spiritual warfare, I began to start dancing, singing, and praising the Lord while in the natural realm, he was dead and had been so for forty-three minutes.

All the staff around me thought I was having a nervous breakdown and that I was crazy and had lost my mind. They could not reason in their minds how a father whose son in the natural realm was dead and could be out there dancing and praising God with the joy of the Lord. However, later, after God raised him from the dead, they could not explain how he came back to life and was not brain-dead like he should have been in the natural realm.

Based on science, being dead that long without adequate oxygen to the brain, even after coming back to life again, he should have been a vegetable. That was another miracle in itself. This was me receiving what Jesus had already paid for, and I did not care about what it may have seemed like in the natural realm.

I was putting God's word in first place, not what I saw in the natural realm. I trusted God that what He had promised me in His word, He was able to perform. Also, my wall of protection and arsenal of weapons that was talked about earlier and were already built up in advance before the battle of that night.

However, if I truly believed that I had received what Jesus already paid for, what action should I have been taking? If I had put what I was seeing in the natural realm in first place instead of giving God's word and His promises first place, what do you think the outcome would have been? He would have died!

The natural realm said he was dead, but God's word promised me my son *"...would have life and have life more abundantly"* (John 10:10 NASB). This is operating in faith 101: put God's word and His promises in first place over anything and everything!

The spiritual supernatural realm supersedes natural law if we are operating in faith in the Kingdom of God by standing on His word and His promises! Jesus commanded us in Matthew 10:8 (KJV) to *"Heal the sick, cleanse the lepers, raise the dead, cast out devils: freely ye have received, freely give."* Jesus would not command us to do something we were not able to do.

Truly, what would have been the outcome if I was out there overwhelmed by fear, crying, screaming, negotiating, and begging God to do something? What if I had not taken authority over the devil's fear? What if I had not confidently, by **faith**, taken authority over death and commanded my son to live in the name of Jesus? What if I was not prepared in advance? He would have died, and it would have been my fault for not applying God's word correctly, not God's.

So, what I am saying is that faith is very simple; man has made it complicated. It does not take any more faith to raise someone from the dead than it does to be cured of a common cold. It does not take an ounce of faith to cure a cold but a ton of faith to raise someone from the dead. They are both easy for

God, and He has already provided and given both in advance and has given you authority over them.

So, God has given you the authority, and you are the one that is going to have to exercise the authority that Jesus paid for at the cross… it is delegated to you. If you are expecting God to delegate the authority He has given you, you are wasting your time. In this case, you are not putting God's word in first place and not appropriately applying God's word. *Again*, if you do not apply God's word correctly, it will not work, and it is your fault, not God's.

Also, it is us blaming God for our failures. We need to free our minds and take the limitations off of God's word and promises by the renewal of our minds. We need to realize that we do not need more **faith**. We just need to use the faith we have already been given effectively by removing unbelief from the faith we do have. I like to say it this way… **faith** is the *absence of unbelief*. This helps me when I feel like my faith is wavering, and it immediately reminds me what I must do. Get in God's word and remove the unbelief that the devil is trying to attach to my faith.

At salvation, each one of us was given *"the measure of faith."* We all get the same amount. It is up to us what we do with it and to feed on God's word and practice it.

> *For I say, through the grace given unto me, to every man that is among you, not to think of himself more highly than he ought to think; but to think soberly, according as God hath dealt to every man the measure of faith.*
>
> — Romans 12:3 (KJV)

God has given us all *"the measure of faith,"* and He does not give someone more than another.

> *And in the morning as they passed by, they saw the fig tree dried up from the roots. And Peter calling to remembrance saith unto him, Master, behold, the fig tree which thou cursedst is withered away. And Jesus answering saith unto them, Have faith in God. For verily I say unto you, That whosoever shall say unto this mountain, Be thou removed, and be thou cast into the sea; and shall not doubt in his heart, but shall believe that those things which he saith shall come to pass; he shall have whatsoever he saith.*
>
> — Mark 11:20–23 (KJV)

I was studying a study guide on this verse, and it said that when Jesus answered, *"Have faith in God,"* and if you take it back to the original Greek, He actually said, *"Have the God kind of* faith.*"* The measure of faith that God gave you is His kind of faith; it is God's **faith** given to you in a measure.

We operate with the **faith of God** that is in us. Now, let's pick something back up that was discussed in an earlier chapter to start putting this all together to renew our minds of who we are in Christ. We learned that our life came out of God's own spirit, and He lives in us. At salvation by the death, burial, and resurrection of the Lord Jesus Christ, Jesus now lives in us by the Holy Spirit.

Also, we have now learned that the **faith of God** lives and operates through us as well. OMG, mic drop… LOL. As a child of God, you have His spirit, life, and authority, and now you just realized you have His **faith**, too! The same **faith** that God used when He said, *Light be,* which lives in you. Hallelujah, glory to God!

You really must comprehend and get revelation knowledge of the point I am trying to make here to renew your mind. As a child of God, you now have God's DNA running through you, just like our children have our DNA. This lines up with God's word when Jesus prayed to God that we would be as one with Him, just like He and the Father are one. What does it mean to be one? This means everything that is in God, Jesus, and the Holy Spirit is also in you. This is huge for the process of renewing your mind.

We think it is only natural and easy for God to operate in the supernatural realm and not be limited by the physical realm. As a child of God, as His legal representative on this earth, you are commissioned and empowered by His authority to do the very same thing! Please, please get this; it is huge. This will free your mind through revelation knowledge to renew your mind so that you can put God's word in first place, apply His word correctly, and take more stock in God's word than what you see in the natural realm, just like God does. This allows you to suspend your human natural reasoning so you can operate in the Kingdom of God through faith just like God does. Glory to God, I just preached myself happy! I am about to jump out of my chair at this moment and just take off on a running spell praising God… LOL.

If we are as one in Christ Jesus, everything that lives in Him now lives in us! We operate in and through the faith of God that was put into us at salvation. Remember, it is not really our lack of faith that keeps us from receiving from God; it is our unbelief caused by lack of knowledge of God's word and His promises of who we are in Christ… that is the problem.

We are children of the most-high God operating in the supernatural realm just like our father, who is God! He commissioned us to do His will on earth just like Jesus was commissioned to do God's will on earth. The only way to remove unbelief is revelation knowledge in God's word and His promises by renewing our minds. This is part of the process of *"be not conformed to this world: but be ye transformed by the renewing of your mind"* (Romans 12:2 KJV).

Faith is actually a noun, and it is believing and unbelieving, which is an action verb on our part. It is a matter of building your **faith** in and on God's word to remove unbelief. The unbelief the devil is trying to deceive us with and fill our **biased mindset** bucket. In every direction possible, the devil is trying to get us to question God's word. In the Garden of Eden, he only had to ask, "Did God say?" The **only** thing he had to do was get man to question God's word.

That is it… that is all he has to do, and it will create unbelief in us. However, here is the good news: it is called the full gospel of Jesus Christ. The word gospel means **good news**. As we study and meditate on God's word, renewing our minds, we get revelation knowledge of who we are in Christ and what all belongs to us as children of God. Then, the devil cannot easily talk us out of everything Jesus paid for us by grace at the cross.

When you receive a revelation of God's word by the Holy Spirit about one of God's promises, the devil will not be able to talk you out of it even if his life depended upon it. When you get revelation knowledge on something, it removes every ounce of unbelief from your faith concerning it, so you can receive it as God intended because God's word is God's will. So, if you are standing on one of God's promises, you are praying in His perfect will.

When we are operating in faith and need something in our lives, we just have to go into God's word and find out where He promises it. Then, find at least three scriptures to back it up. 2 Corinthians 13:1(KJV) says, *"with the mouth of two or three witnesses may every word be established."* Then, just meditate (renew your mind) on God's word concerning what you are believing for, and it removes the unbelief so that you can receive it through your **faith**. That same measure of faith was given to us in the same measure as everybody else.

Isn't it exciting to know that you are capable of doing great feats of faith because you are just as equipped as everyone else is? Glory to God! We are given the same measure of faith as the apostle Paul and every other child of God before us. So, we have to ask ourselves, if we are not walking and operating in the same power that the apostle Paul operated in, where are we missing it, and where has the devil deceived us?

And here is the clue: *"Peter said, Silver and gold have I none; but such as I have give I thee: In the name of Jesus Christ of Nazareth rise up and walk"* (Acts 3:6 KJV). What did Peter have that he could give away? He understood the authority in the name of Jesus that was in him because of the life of God that lived inside of him. He understood through revelation knowledge by the renewing of his mind that he was one with Christ and that what was in Jesus was now in him. And just like Jesus, he was doing God's will on earth, in the name of Jesus. We are empowered and commanded to do the same.

You must comprehend through revelation knowledge that God has already given you everything, and all you have to do is receive what He has already promised, paid for, and has already given you in His word. God's word is God's will! However, it does take renewing your mind by receiving revelation knowledge of God's word of who you are in Christ and what He has already given to you. Then, you can stand on your faith in God's word with all unbelief removed, which is faith in operation as God designed it. Equally as important, you must have that settled in your spirit long before a battle, not during one.

The number one thing you must do at the very onset of an attack is to **control your emotions.** The Bible tells us how and where faith comes from and how to receive it. Romans 10v17 (KJV)says, *"So then faith cometh by hearing, and hearing by the word of God."* I like the way it repeated the word "hearing" twice in that verse. So, we could also say it like this… *"Faith cometh by hearing and hearing and hearing and hearing by the word of God."*

- How do we learn anything in the natural realm?
- How much learning and training does it take to become a doctor, lawyer, professional athlete, or diesel mechanic?
- How much effort and volunteering of your time and activities does it take to achieve them?

Many are willing to spend hundreds of thousands of dollars on an education and spend from four to twelve years of their life in school to accomplish it. And yet, it is not even close to having the value and power of knowing who you are in Christ.

We only need an education for a fraction of the time compared to eternity. The good news is that we can learn **faith** quicker than we can for most professions. However, it does take the dedication of our time, effort, and practice to accomplish it like anything else does.

Let's go back to the beginning because **faith** is very simple. Faith is just putting God's word in first place over what you see in the natural realm. Faith is just the absence of unbelief, and there is no unbelief attached to your **faith**. Remember, God has given us all the same measure of **faith**. How we make the **faith** that God gave us productive is to remove the unbelief, the deception that the devil will try to attach to it, and feed on the word of God and His promises.

Remember, the devil does not have to get you to disbelieve God's word and His promises; all he has to do is get you to question God's word and His promises. Because if he can only get you to question God's word, he automatically gets unbelief that he can attach to our **faith** to defeat you and make your **faith** nonproductive.

We must apply God's word correctly by giving God's word first place over anything we see in the natural realm. As we build ourselves up with revelation knowledge from God's word and these *Five Simple Truths*, the devil does not stand a chance against us. Because we are operating on our faith without unbelief attached to it. This is the way faith was designed to work and the way God created it to work. Faith is now. If it is not now, then it is not faith. Again…

> *Now faith is the substance of things hoped for, the evidence things not seen.*
>
> — Hebrews 11:1 (KJV)

As I mentioned, we have to renew our minds on how to start thinking and believing in the spiritual realm. In and on God's word and His promises by putting His word in first place over anything we can sense in the natural realm. Again, stop being dominated in the flesh by the devil in the natural and emotional realm.

Once our minds are renewed, we no longer think through the flesh and will not be limited by the five physical senses in the natural realm. We can see and experience miracles, which are God's word and His promises coming to reality into the natural realm. We start thinking and operating like God in the supernatural spiritual realm. Not bound or limited to what we can see through our five physical senses in the natural realm. We are operating in the supernatural realm by **faith**, pulling things that have already been given to us by God in His word and promises that exist in the spiritual realm. When we put God's word in first place, not by what we see in the natural realm based on our five physical senses... we are operating in the Kingdom of God through faith, and nothing is impossible to us. We are capable of operating on this earth, just like Jesus did. By grace, we are His legal representatives on this earth, and we operate through and by **faith**.

Faith is the greatest gift that God gave us, and He expects us to use it to operate in the supernatural spiritual realm and to fellowship with Him. Faith is the most important subject in the Bible. You cannot be saved without it, you cannot fellowship with God without it, you cannot operate in the Kingdom of God the way God intended for you to, and you can never please God without it.

> *"Without faith it is impossible to please God!"*
> — Hebrews 11:6 (KJV)

CHAPTER 6

The Five Simple Truths—Second… Jesus

In the beginning was the Word, and the Word was with God and the Word was God.

— John 1:1 (KJV)

And the Word was made flesh, and dwelt among us, (and we beheld his glory, the glory as of the only begotten of the Father,) full of grace and truth.

— John 1:14 (KJV)

Jesus said unto them, Verily, verily, I say unto you, Before Abraham was, I am.

— John 8:58 (KJV)

Jesus was part of the Trinity (Father, Son, and the Holy Spirit) before the world began, but they are one and the same. Sometimes, the Trinity can be complicated for us to comprehend. Let's use water as a comparison. You have water, ice, and moisture vapor, but they are all water in different states of being and operate differently in each form. Jesus was *"the lamb slain from the foundation of the world."*

> *And all that dwell upon the earth shall worship him, whose names are not written in the book of life of "the Lamb slain from the foundation of the world.*
>
> — Revelation 13:8 (KJV)

There was so much prophecy about the Messiah and how He would come, what He would accomplish, and what would happen to Him. Every prophecy is picture-perfect of who Jesus was and what He did at the cross. Every prophecy given about the Messiah and what would happen to Him was accomplished by the life, death, burial, and resurrection of the Lord Jesus Christ. Jesus fulfilled all the prophecies given concerning the Messiah to the letter. For example,

> *Who hath believed our report? and to whom is the arm of the LORD revealed? For he shall grow up before him as a tender plant, and as a root out of a dry ground: he hath no form nor comeliness; and when we shall see him, there is no beauty that we should desire him. He is despised and rejected of men; a man of sorrows, and acquainted with grief: and we hid as it were our faces from him; he was despised, and we esteemed him not. Surely he hath borne our griefs, and carried our sorrows: yet we did esteem him stricken, smitten of God, and afflicted. But he was wounded for our transgressions, he was bruised for our iniquities: the chastisement of our peace was upon him; and*

with his stripes we are healed. All we like sheep have gone astray; we have turned everyone to his own way; and the L<small>ORD</small> *hath laid on him the iniquity of us all. He was oppressed, and he was afflicted, yet he opened not his mouth: he is brought as a lamb to the slaughter, and as a sheep before her shearers is dumb, so he openeth not his mouth. He was taken from prison and from judgment: and who shall declare his generation? for he was cut off out of the land of the living: for the transgression of my people was he stricken. And he made his grave with the wicked, and with the rich in his death; because he had done no violence, neither was any deceit in his mouth. Yet it pleased the* L<small>ORD</small> *to bruise him; he hath put him to grief: when thou shalt make his soul an offering for sin, he shall see his seed, he shall prolong his days, and the pleasure of the Lord shall prosper in his hand. He shall see of the travail of his soul, and shall be satisfied: by his knowledge shall my righteous servant justify many; for he shall bear their iniquities. Therefore will I divide him a portion with the great, and he shall divide the spoil with the strong; because he hath poured out his soul unto death: and he was numbered with the transgressors; and he bare the sin of many, and made intercession for the transgressors.*

— Isaiah 53:1–12 (KJV)

Here was the problem… man was looking for an earthly messiah to come, dominate, and operate in the physical realm. They were looking for a messiah who would come in and take on the Roman Empire in the natural realm. Meanwhile, the Messiah that God was giving, as was prophesied, was someone who would dominate and operate in the Kingdom of God in the spiritual realm. Also, to redeem man from the fall in the Garden of Eden. This was a thousand times more important and would last for eternity.

So, a messiah was needed, but not a messiah who would just come in and take care of a temporary situation over a puny king at only one period of time in history. What the Messiah paid for us in the supernatural spiritual realm was way more important than some stupid king at that time. He came back and paid for the right for us to become the sons of God like He truly intended, as He did with Adam before the fall of men.

Everything that is discussed in this book is what the Messiah paid for on our behalf. He has already paid for every sin we have ever committed or ever will. He has given God's children their ability to fellowship and operate with Him directly in the spiritual realm in and through our spirit, where He now lives by faith. Jesus was God.

> *Philip said to Him, "Lord, show us the Father, and it is sufficient for us."*
>
> *Jesus said to him, "Have I been with you so long, and yet you have not known Me, Philip? He who has seen Me has seen the Father; so how can you say, 'Show us the Father'"?*
>
> — John 14:8–9 (NKJV)

So, Jesus was God, and He said so in the verse above. Jesus was and still is our Messiah and is the son of God.

My heart breaks for my Jewish and Muslim brothers and sisters. Their messiah is staring them right in the face in all of the prophecies right before their eyes. This book is not intended to **make a case for Christ**. That would take a whole book in itself. However, if you are reading this book and you are not sure that Jesus is your Messiah, I implore you to do deeper research on your own. If you can temporarily suspend your old, biased mindset of all that you have possibly been indoctrinated in and ask God for wisdom, He will reveal Himself to you.

God loves you, and He wants you to receive wisdom even more than you do. If what you believe is true, then that truth can stand to be challenged. If it cannot, it was not the truth to start with. However, if **truth** is what you seek, then both theories should be given an equal amount of time for research if you are sincere and want to know the truth, whatever it is.

Remember, God loves you, and He wants an intimate relationship with you. He says, *if we seek Him with our whole hearts, we will find Him.*

> *And ye shall seek me, and find me, when ye shall search for me with all your heart.*
>
> — Jeremiah 29:13 (KJV)

As a born-again child of God, I know that Jesus paid it all for me at the cross and that my name is written down in the Lamb's Book of Life by the **Lamb of God** who was *"slain from the foundation of the world"* (Revelation 13:8 KJV). I already have guaranteed acceptance into Heaven forever with God despite my flaws that Jesus so graciously paid for on my behalf at the cross. You can also have that confident assurance in your spirit of salvation, knowing you will live with your heavenly father for eternity in Heaven. There is no way to earn it! You cannot earn that through the old law or by seeing if your works are good enough to get you into Heaven.

I could not imagine a life where I did not know for sure if my works were good enough to get me into Heaven. If God is the God of love and your father, and He is, why would He make His children strive their whole life to be good and still possibly send them to hell? Even an earthly father with all his flaws would not do something this evil to his children, and neither would God. Salvation is a free gift from God, who offered His son to reconcile man back to Him. This is what our Messiah, the Lord Jesus Christ, did at the cross by paying for all our sins through our salvation by grace… Glory to God!

God had a plan of salvation before the world even began. Jesus was *"The lamb slain from the foundation of the world."* He knew if He gave man free will that we would fail Him at some point. However, He wanted to give us free will because you cannot have an intimate relationship with someone unless they choose you with their own free will. It would be the difference between having a wife versus a slave girl down in the basement.

In Revelation, Jesus actually calls us *"His bride."* (Revelation 19:7 NIV). So, in essence, He had already planned to sacrifice Himself (Jesus) on the cross for the relationship He so desired to have with us. He sacrificed His own self for us because He loved us that much.

In the Old Testament, they made sacrifices to cover the sins of the people. However, that was a shadow and type of what would come through the Messiah, Jesus. Then God took on flesh (in the form of Jesus) to give the ultimate sacrifice at the cross for us so that He could move out of temples on earth and actually move **back** into us, in our spirit that we lost at the fall of man. The same way He did with the original man, Adam. His ultimate sacrifice did away with the old law, the curses, and the sacrifices that applied to it. These sacrifices only covered the sins; they did not remove our sins.

God has been in our spirits since conception, but at the age of accountability, at some point, we sinned, and that part of our spirits died spiritually. However, when we accept Christ as our savior, God comes back into us, in our spirits.

After dark one night a Jewish religious leader named Nicodemus, a member of the sect of the Pharisees, came for an interview with Jesus. "Sir," he said, "we all know that God has sent you to teach us. Your miracles are proof enough of this."

Jesus replied, "With all the earnestness I possess I tell you this: Unless you are born again, you can never get into the Kingdom of God."

"Born again!" exclaimed Nicodemus. "What do you mean? How can an old man go back into his mother's womb and be born again?"

Jesus replied, "What I am telling you so earnestly is this: Unless one is born of water and the Spirit, he cannot enter the Kingdom of God. Men can only reproduce human life, but the Holy Spirit gives new life from heaven; so don't be surprised at my statement that you must be born again! Just as you can hear the wind but can't tell where it comes from or where it will go next, so it is with the Spirit. We do not know on whom he will next bestow this life from heaven."

"What do you mean?" Nicodemus asked.

Jesus replied, "You, a respected Jewish teacher, and yet you don't understand these things? I am telling you what I know and have seen—and yet you won't believe me. But if you don't even believe me when I tell you about such things as these that happen here among men, how can you possibly believe if I tell you what is going on in heaven? For only I, the Messiah, have come to earth and will return to heaven again. And as Moses in the wilderness lifted up the bronze image of a serpent on a pole, even so I must be lifted up upon a pole, so that anyone who believes in me will have eternal life. For God loved the world so much that he gave his only Son so that anyone who believes in him shall not perish but have eternal life. God did not send his Son into the world to condemn it, but to save it.

"There is no eternal doom awaiting those who trust him to save them. But those who don't trust him have already been tried and condemned for not believing in the only Son of God. Their sentence is based on this fact: that the Light from heaven came into the world, but they loved the darkness more than the Light, for their deeds were evil. They hated the heavenly Light because they wanted to sin in the darkness. They stayed away from that Light for fear their sins would be exposed and they would be punished. But those doing right come gladly to the

> *Light to let everyone see that they are doing what God wants them to."*
>
> — John 3:1–21 (TLB)

That is being **born again.** Jesus paid the ultimate sacrifice to remove the curse of the law and wash away and **remove** every sin we ever have committed or will ever commit.

The curtain surrounding the "Ark of the Covenant" (the Mercy Seat) in the inner temple in Jerusalem was seven inches thick. It is recorded that the moment when Jesus died on the cross, the **curtain was ripped from top to bottom.**

> *And, behold, the veil of the temple was rent in twain from the top to the bottom; and the earth did quake, and the rocks rent;*
>
> — Matthew 27:51 (KJV)

God busted out of there and moved back into His earthly temple in us, in our spirits, where He lived before the fall of man in the Garden of Eden.

> *For if by one man's offence death reigned by one; much more they which receive abundance of grace and of the gift of righteousness shall reign in life by one, Jesus Christ.*
>
> — Romans 5:17 (KJV)

Sometimes, we may wonder how a single sacrifice can justify us all, forever, for everything and anything. It is very important to read Romans 5:12–21 because it puts everything into perspective. Jesus is also known as the second Adam. So with one man, Adam brought sin and condemnation upon all of creation, our bodies, our spirits, and even the planet Earth itself, which was also corrupted.

How much more can one man, Jesus, rectify all of creation back to God?

Why is it easy for us to think that one man, Adam, could cause the fall of all but struggle to comprehend that one man, Jesus, can justify us all?

So, when we can comprehend who we are in Christ, we must see what God sees. When He sees us, He sees Jesus. Jesus came to live in our spirits, and we are His legal representative on this earth.

Now, let's look at another aspect of **faith** that came into place after the sacrifice of Jesus for the body of Christ. He took up new residence in us, in our spirits, when we accepted Him as our savior. When Jesus was on the earth, the Bible says that *the power was there to heal them.*

> *Now it happened on a certain day, as He was teaching, that there were Pharisees and teachers of the law sitting by, who had come out of every town of Galilee, Judea, and Jerusalem. And the power of the Lord was present to heal them.*
>
> — Luke 5:17 (NKJV)

Everywhere Jesus went, He healed everybody that came to Him. There is not a single instance in the Bible where anyone came to Jesus for healing that He did not heal them. He healed them all, every time, in every case, without discrimination. Only the Son of God, who was God, would have been able to do that. So, Jesus was God, and God showed His character and His will that everyone should receive healing.

Jesus paid the price for all of us and for all the things we lost with the fall of man. This paid for the salvation of all, and Jesus paid for the healing of all. When I say all, I mean all. Let me give you an example of this truth.

I have heard so many exciting testimonies like this, but I will just give you one as an example. They all pretty much happened when someone received revelation knowledge that Jesus is the healer. It is when I hear so many wonderful testimonies about Muslims and Jewish brothers and sisters receiving healing when they receive revelation knowledge about Jesus, a prophet, by their admission. Even in the Quran, they called Him a prophet and a healer. Our Muslim and Jewish brothers and sisters have received miraculous miracle healing by calling on the name of Jesus.

When people see testimonies with their own eyes of the children of God receiving miraculous healing in the name of Jesus… they realize this same Jesus is also in their book. When someone is desperate for healing, their faith is fertile ground for hearing the truth for themselves that Jesus was and still is their healer. Not a single person that Jesus healed while He was on this earth was a Christian, yet.

Let that sink in for a moment as it messes up all your theology… LOL. Sometimes, when I am praying about something, I get a feeling of condemnation and that I am unworthy even to receive what I am praying for or have authority over something the devil is trying to do in my life. However, that is the devil who is condemning me. Then, I just remind myself that I am not operating on my authority and righteousness. I am operating with Jesus' authority and His righteousness.

This is very important to understand because the devil will use condemnation against you to make you ineffective. When I find myself in spiritual warfare, I remind the devil of this out loud with my words that the words I am decreeing have the same power and authority as if the words actually came out of the actual mouth of God. In reality, they did because I am in Christ, and Christ is in me, and He operates through me. I am speaking the word of God, which is His will, with the authority of the Lord Jesus Christ, and God's word will not come back void.

If the devil can condemn you and make you think that you have to be perfect to exercise authority on this earth, he will deceive you and strip you of all your authority. If we could only exercise our authority in Christ when we are perfect, then not a single person would ever be able to accomplish anything on this earth for God. Because we are all imperfect, we have all sinned and fallen short of the glory of God. If God's will could only be exercised on this earth through someone who is perfect, then God's will would never be able to be performed here after Jesus' death. The death, burial, and resurrection of the Lord Jesus Christ would have been an absolute failure, and we know that is not the case.

So, you have to understand, especially in spiritual warfare, that you are not standing on your righteousness or your authority. You are exercising Jesus' authority through and on His righteousness. Again, you are speaking God's word and His promises, and He said His word would not come back void. As a child of God speaking God's word, which is His perfect will, has the same power as if it came out of His own mouth.

> *Because as he [Jesus] is, so are we in this world.*
> — 1 John 4:17b (KJV)

Praise the Lord! We are the same as Jesus in this world; we are His legal representative on this earth. Just let that sink into your (soul) mind. Spend some time meditating on that truth alone, and your flesh and old mindset will start being renewed. When you get true revelation knowledge of what Christ has done for you, the fact that He lives in you… then you will see that we are equipped to operate on this earth the same way he was. Not because of who we are but because of who lives in us.

> *And God raised [past tense] us up with Christ and seated (past tense) us with him in the heavenly realms in Christ Jesus.*
> — Ephesians 2:6 (NIV)

Look where you now sit. You sit and operate in the supernatural spiritual realm with Christ Jesus in the heavenly realm. When you can understand who you are in Christ, you can divert the darts of faith-destroying condemnation that the devil will throw at you.

> *For if by one man's offence death reigned by one; much more they which receive abundance of grace and of*

> *the gift of righteousness shall reign in life by one, Jesus Christ.*
>
> — Romans 5:17 (KJV)

What does it mean to reign in life through Jesus Christ? Romans 5:17 reveals to what extent God has gone to provide us with authority over the kingdom of darkness. The life He wants for every believer is one in which each believer *"reigns in life."*

Reign means to exert "dominion or exercise authority."[5] Believers are to live a life in which we exert dominion by taking authority over the devil and anything he would try and put on us. At salvation, God removed our guilt and sin and placed upon us Jesus' robe of righteousness by grace (not works). The definition of grace is "unmerited favor."[6] So, if we receive this authority and dominion by grace, then it is not how good we are or how perfect our good works are because they never will be. It is based on what Jesus did.

Remember, when you are exercising authority over the devil it is based on Jesus' righteousness and His authority, not yours. Remember, He has given you the grace to do so on His behalf, not based on how good you are but based on what He did at the cross on our behalf. Thus, we received it by grace, through **faith** in Him and on God's word and His promises.

---

5 "Reign," Merriam-Webster Online Dictionary. Merriam-Webster, Incorporated, July 3, 2024, https://www.merriam-webster.com/dictionary/reign.

6 "Grace," Oxford English Dictionary, 2024, https://www.oed.com/dictionary/grace_n.

> *"In solemn truth I tell you, anyone believing in me [he did not say anyone how was perfect or without sin] shall do the same miracles I have done, and even greater ones, because I am going to be with the Father. You can ask him for anything, using my name, and I will do it, this will bring praise to the Father because of what I, the Son will do for you. Yes, ask anything, using my name, and I will do it!*
>
> — John 14:12–14 (TLB)

The disciples knew that Jesus would never lie to them, yet He still wanted to make absolutely sure to get His point across strongly by saying, *"In solemn truth."* He also used this phrase in Mark 11:23 when He was telling us that they could speak to the mountain and tell it to be cast in the sea, and it would go. Most people struggle with the fact that we are capable of doing what Jesus did. One can only imagine doing greater miracles than Jesus did, though it says it here clearly in the Bible.

So, when Jesus was on the earth, this power was only on Him. However, now, after the death, burial, and resurrection of the Lord Jesus Christ, we are His legal representative on this earth, as imperfect as we are. Anywhere a child of God is, there is Jesus.

> *Heal the sick, cleanse the lepers, raise the dead, cast out devils: freely ye have received, freely give.*
>
> — Matthew 10:8 (KJV)

This was Jesus Himself giving instructions to the body of Christ. He **gave** us something. What did He give us? His authority! What are we supposed to do with it? *"Freely give"* (action verb), heal the sick, raise the dead, and exercise our authority over the kingdom of darkness. What a gift! Glory to God! He gave us this authority in His name based on His righteousness, not ours, and He has commanded us to exercise it for the Kingdom of God while we are on this earth. Peter and John gave a perfect example for us as the body of Christ.

> *Then Peter said, "Silver and gold I do not have, but what I do have I give you: In the name of Jesus Christ of Nazareth, rise up and walk."*
>
> — Acts 3: 6 (NKJV)

They were given something, and they were giving it away. They had received the authority of the name of Jesus and were exercising it by *giving what they had received!* Also, notice they did not pray for or over him, nor did they start a prayer chain on social media. LOL. They simply exercised their authority and commanded him to walk in the name of Jesus. They did not pray to God and ask God to heal him. They simply spoke directly to the problem by **faith** in the authority of the name of Jesus!

I am going to take a little side journey here for a moment because this is the perfect place to comprehend one of the biggest mistakes that the Body of Christ makes concerning operating in **faith** and authority. A good example to illustrate this is healing, but it applies to everything that Jesus paid for on the cross.

The average Christian prays to God about their problem when He has already given them the authority in the name of Jesus to do it for themselves. God gave you something, and He expects you to use it and not waste His time or yours by not applying God's word correctly. Trying to get Him to do something He has already done and told you to do something about. God already did His part; He gave you His word, His promises, and the authority of the name of Jesus.

So here is an example of a wrong way to pray about healing: "Dear gracious heavenly father, I pray that you will heal my back from all the pain." Now, the correct way… "Pain, I command you to leave my body in the name of Jesus!"

We are supposed to speak directly to our problem with our authority about our God, not talking to God about our problem. If we want God's word to work, **that will not come back void**; we have to apply it correctly.

Now, back to the subject of Jesus. So, now, instead of only having Jesus exercising His authority on this earth, He can be anywhere a child of God is.

> *I never stopped thanking God for you. I pray for you constantly, asking God, the glorious Father of our Lord Jesus Christ, to give you wisdom to see clearly and really understand who Christ is and all that he has done for you. I pray that your hearts will be flooded with light [revelation knowledge] so that you can see something of the future he has called you to share. I want you to realize that God has been made rich because we who are in Christ's have been given to him! I pray that you begin to understand how*

> *incredibly great his power is to help those who believe in him. It is that same mighty power that raised Christ from the dead and seated him in the place of honor at God's right hand in heaven, far, far above any other king or ruler or dictator or leader. Yes, his honor is far more glorious than that of anyone else either in the world or in the world to come. And God has put all things under his feet and made him the supreme Head of the Church—which is his body, filled with himself, and the Author and Giver of everything everywhere.*
>
> — Ephesians 1:16–23 (TLB)

So, when I read that God had become rich because of me, I kind of struggled with that because I thought it was the other way around, and that is enormously true. Then I realized that instead of one person on this earth, Jesus performed God's will and authority for His people. Now, everyone who is a born-again child of God can do the same things for Him and for themselves on this earth that Jesus did for Him on this earth.

However, each person has their part to play. God gave you authority purchased by Jesus at the cross. Then He robed you with His authority and righteousness and commanded you to go out and defeat the kingdom of darkness. God did this not just for your life but for the people that are around you so that will draw them to Christ.

Read through the first four gospels in the Bible about Jesus while He was on this earth. As you are reading through it and everywhere you see a miracle or healing take place, ask yourself this question. Was it Jesus' faith that healed, or was it the individual's faith that healed them? In doing so, you will see how they both, in most cases, worked together. In Jesus' own hometown, it said, *"And he could there do no mighty work, save that he laid his hands upon a few sick folk, and healed them. And he marveled because of their unbelief. And he went round about the villages, teaching"* (Mark 6:5–6 KJV).

So, their **unbelief** even hindered Jesus from performing mighty healings and miracles. This does not contradict what I said earlier that you cannot find a single place in the Bible where someone came to Jesus for healing that He did not heal them. Only the Messiah, Son of God who was God, could have done this.

CHAPTER 7

The Five Simple Truths—Third… Seed Time and Harvest

If you will notice in the Bible, many of Jesus' sermons compared life to **sowing a seed** and the type of seed and soil you sow determines your harvest.

> *And he spake many things unto them in parables, saying, Behold, a sower went forth to sow; And when he sowed, some seeds fell by the way side, and the fowls came and devoured them up: Some fell upon stony places, where they had not much earth: and forthwith they sprung up, because they had no deepness of earth: And when the sun was up, they were scorched; and because they had no root, they withered away. And some fell among thorns; and the thorns sprung up, and choked them: But other fell into good ground, and*

brought forth fruit, some an hundredfold, some sixtyfold, some thirtyfold.

— Matthew 13:3–9 (KJV)

This is **seed time and harvest**, and we determined *"some a hundredfold, some sixtyfold, some thirtyfold"* based on how we take care of the seed of God's word that was planted in our hearts. The seed discussed in this scripture is the seed of God's word and what kind of soil in which it is planted.

Your soul (mind) is the garden in which God's word is planted. However, it is up to you to take care of that seed in that garden. Plus, you determine how fertile and productive it is. For just a brief analogy, let's think about a garden for a moment to show its simplicity. You cannot just sow a seed in a garden and then come back in the fall and see how it turned out. You have to plant that seed; you have to water it on a daily basis, fertilize it, and guard it against birds and pests trying to destroy it. You also have to keep all the weeds pulled out of it so that it does not get choked out until the harvest comes.

I planted a garden once, and this parable came as revelation knowledge to me. Preparing and planting that seed in that garden was not the hardest part. It was caring for and protecting it on a daily basis, which was the objective if I wanted to have a successful harvest. Then, I truly realized what the Lord Jesus Christ was talking about in that parable. I spent more time caring for and protecting that garden than I did the actual planning of it. Halfway through the growing season, I even started to question how badly I wanted that garden. Plus, that is the way the devil is with the seed of God's word in our hearts.

So, when we plant a seed of God's word about something we are praying for, we have to water it daily with God's word and His promises. We must fertilize it with praise and worship. We have to keep all the pests and the weeds, which are fear, worry, doubt, and unbelief, out and off of that seed until we receive the harvest through and by our faith in God's word and His promises.

But another extremely important seed to consider is our words. Every word that we let come out of our mouths is a seed that we plant, and at some point, we will reap the harvest. Let's go back to the story of Job for a moment… What seed (word) did Job plant? He planted words of **fear and worry** about all the things he was afraid would come upon him, and he received that harvest.

Once he planted those words (seeds), the harvest came for the type of seed he planted. That is what was going on between God and satan. Satan came to collect the harvest of the seeds Job planted. Except, God limited what satan could do to Job based on the seed that he planted and was not allowed to go beyond.

God is bound by His own word, and He cannot lie. He set the foundation of the spiritual law of seed time and harvest (blessing and curses), and satan came for the seed that Job planted.

So, when we understand that every word that comes out of our mouth is a seed, we need to be very mindful of the words we speak. They are as powerful as if they came out of the very mouth of God, which is the reality of it if delivered in **faith**. Also, everything God says comes to pass at some time without exception. God said **His word would not come back void** (Isaiah 55:11).

When you speak God's word, it will not come back void. As a child of God with Him living on the inside of us, potentially every word that comes out of our mouths has the same power as if it came out of the mouth of God. Because, in essence, it did… because He lives in us and operates through us on this earth.

For instance, if you are praying for healing, you cannot speak words of doubt, unbelief, or fear. That does not mean that these thoughts do not come into our minds, but we have the choice whether or not they become a seed by listening to satan's lies, and then we actually release them out loud with our words into the earth. You cannot keep a bird from flying over your head, but you have the choice of whether or not you are going to let him build a nest on it.

This can be very challenging when we are not feeling good and someone asks us how we are doing. Especially if you are going to the doctor and he asks you these types of questions. You have to answer them based on what is going on in the natural realm. It is very hard in the natural not to take the victim's mentality and control the emotion of wanting to receive pity. In these cases, at least finish your sentence out with something like this, "But in the name of Jesus, I am healed," or at least "I will feel better," etc. Consciously try your best to never leave a negative seed (word) unchecked without replacing it with a positive one of the desired outcomes based on God's word and His promises. Just think of your words as bullets, and every time you speak them out, you pull the trigger.

We need to speak (plant a seed) faith-filled, positive words of our desired outcome of what we are believing God for based on God's word and His promises. And not what we might see in the physical realm with our five senses at that time. This is the essence of seed time and harvest. You must understand that your **faith** is based on what you cannot see, not what you can see. If you can see it, it is not faith. We must give God's word and His promises first place over anything we see or feel with our physical senses.

In this case, we are putting God's word in first place by having faith in God's word and His promises *"by whose stripes ye were healed"* (1 Peter 2:24 KJV) and not what we might see physically in the natural realm. Then, you start praising God for what you already believe you have received before you ever see it manifest in the natural realm. It is not the other way around, where you are not applying God's word correctly, and it will not work.

I use the verse above a lot because it is short for the purpose of writing. However, God's word is loaded with healing scriptures that you can stand on for the basis of your healing. I have learned in some bad situations when it looked so overwhelming, where I was devastated and could not conjure up faith-filled positive words at that moment, that if I would at least **keep my big mouth shut** and not release the negative words, it was enough to win that battle by not sowing a seed of failure with my words in that situation.

This is part of controlling your emotions. There may have been a battle going on in my mind where the devil was raging war with me, but I learned to **keep my big mouth shut**. At least until I could build my faith back up on God's word and

His promises to get back in the fight. Also, think of it this way. If you planted a seed, would you dig it up out of the ground every day to see if it is growing? Of course not; you will kill the seed, and it could never grow.

So, once we sow a seed of faith to receive something God has already promised and given us in His word, we just need to have faith that it is growing. At some point in time, the seed we planted will eventually emerge into a beautiful harvest of what we planted and desired. Also, we must protect that seed until the harvest comes by removing the fear and worry, which manifests as unbelief. We need to nourish it with God's word and His promises, which remove unbelief and takes care of that seed until the harvest comes.

This is God's spiritual law and government. This is where we see how **faith** and seed time and harvest work in unison with each other. Even in a true battle situation that could be a spontaneous attack from the devil, we can still use the spiritual law of seed time and harvest. This is where it is important to pray and decree things like Psalm 91 and the Ephesians prayer over yourself and your family on a regular basis. You will have a seed of God's word that you have already planted to stand on in that battle at a moment's notice when the devil attacks. More importantly, like I have said more than once, it is still a lot more effective to have already done this in advance and be prepared for a battle long before the devil ever shows up at your gate by using the spiritual law of seed time and harvest with God word as God intended.

Let's finish by talking about finances when it comes to seed time and harvest. I like to say, "If God can get it through you, He will get it to you." We are kind of like a funnel that God uses. If we clog it up and let nothing through, everything just spills out and goes to waste, and everyone involved ends up with nothing! Then, the devil gets to kill, steal, and destroy your finances (John 10:10).

You can use this process of thinking about everything you desire from God based on His word and His promises. If you need finances, then you sow a financial seed by letting it go through you like a funnel into someone else so that God can pour more finances into your funnel (seed time and harvest). Everybody wants to learn how to receive and praise the Lord, and it is very easy to learn how to do—just give! You cannot receive a harvest from the Kingdom of God if you do not plant a seed into it. This is seed time and harvest 101. "*…some a hundredfold, some sixtyfold, some thirtyfold*" (Matthew 13:9 KJV). This would be like fantasyland to Wall Street.

I do not want to turn this book into a prosperity message, but I will say this to testify to this truth: God is no respecter of persons. When I applied the *Five Simple Truths*, with seed time and harvest being one of them, God honored His word and blessed me beyond my wildest imagination. I am not bragging about myself because I probably still limited Him to what He truly wanted to do. The spiritual truth of seed time and harvest is so vital because this truth is the most consistent common denominator in all five of the *Five Simple Truths*.

CHAPTER 8

The Five Simple Truths—Fourth... Forgiveness

There is only one thing that will keep us from receiving forgiveness, and that is for us not to forgive.

> *For if you forgive other people when they sin against you, your heavenly Father will also forgive you. But if you do not forgive others their sins, your father will not forgive your sins.*
>
> — Matthew 6:14–15 (NIV)

We could easily find several scriptures that say the very same thing. I used to have the worst problem with this. Forgiving people almost seemed impossible for me, and I had the ability to hold a grudge forever. Then, one day, the Holy Spirit showed me something through revelation knowledge, and now it has turned into the easiest thing for me to do in my Christian walk.

There are two things that will absolutely block every prayer you have, and that is unbelief and unforgiveness. Kenneth E.

Hagin once said in one of his sermons I had listened to that when people came to him and asked why their faith was not working, and he always checked these two areas. And 99% of the time, it was one of the two or a combination of both. I found this to be true in my own life as well.

If I am praying about something important to me, is unforgiveness worth destroying it? My most favorite verse in the Bible is Mark 11:23. The holy spirit even inspired me to write a song about it, and it is on my YouTube channel.

> *For verily I say unto you, that whosoever shall say unto this mountain, Be thou removed, and be thou cast into the sea; and shall not doubt in his heart, but shall believe that those things which he saith shall come to pass; he shall have whatsoever he saith. Therefore I say unto you, what things soever ye desire, when ye pray, [not when you see it with your five physical senses], believe that ye receive them, and ye shall have them.*
>
> — Mark 11:23–24 (KJV)

But then the Lord had to go and put verse 25 in that followed verse 24, which just messed everything up… LOL.

> *And when ye stand praying, forgive, if ye have ought against any: that your Father also which is in heaven may forgive you your trespasses.*
>
> — Mark 11:25 (KJV)

So, this meant if I wanted to have and operate in verses 23 and 24, I also had to do verse 25. This gave me the motivation to start learning how to forgive. I was faced with the reality that if I could not learn how to forgive, then I could not be forgiven or operate in everything that His word said I could operate in. And with anything, the more you practice something, the easier it becomes.

Here is just a side note about this verse concerning our words. Notice in these verses how many times He used the word *"saith."* That is faith and seed time and harvest working together in unison. Also, notice in verse 24, where you see the word *"say"* or *"saith,"* which means when you know what God's will is concerning something that is based on God's word and His promises, like healing, for instance, you do not have to pray it. You can decree it with your words in the name of Jesus right to the devil's face based on God's word and His promises.

I like what Andrew Womack said about this verse when I was falling asleep one night while listening to one of his sermons. He mentioned that most people did just the opposite of what this verse instructed us to do. Most people speak to God about **their** mountain, but we are supposed to speak directly to our mountain **about our God**! We are supposed to speak God's words and His promises with our authority that Jesus paid for directly to our mountain, not to God. We are the ones who are supposed to do something about that mountain, not God; He has already done His part. He gave us His word, His promises, and the authority to speak to our mountain directly in His name. God's word will work perfectly through and by our **faith** if we apply His word correctly.

If you are begging God to do something about your mountain, you are not applying the word correctly, and it will not work. When it does not work, it is not God's fault; it is our fault for not applying His word correctly as He commissioned it. Forgive me… I got excited and off subject… LOL. Let's get back to forgiveness.

Anytime you pray about something, in the back of your mind, you should always be asking yourself if there is anyone you have not forgiven. This is not in a judgmental way; it is just always checking up in our spirits to make sure there is no unforgiveness within us as just part of an everyday fellowship with God.

Jesus will forgive you for anything. We must do the same. If you have a problem in this area, just start praying for that person until you believe it. You may not have your complete heart in it when you start, just do it as an act of obedience. Forgiveness is also an act of faith; it may not be a reality at the moment in your mind (soul), but it will eventually come to pass if you are obedient.

I have found it virtually impossible to pray for someone without the love of God rising up in me and the unforgiveness to start melting away. That is how I know I can stop praying for them when the unforgiveness has left. Until that unforgiveness has left you, you keep praying for them until it does.

Remember, Jesus died for their mistakes just like He did for yours. He loves them just like He does you. They just yielded to the wrong spirit when they sinned against you, just like you do when you sin against God. Are we truly any better than they are? Have we all not sinned and fallen short of the glory of God? Is there really a grudge so important to you that it is worth blocking all your prayers, healing, and blessings? They control your life and your prayers for the cheap cost of a petty grudge. This is a trap from the devil. Who in this situation has the greater loss? They get free rent in your head and destroy all your joy as well as your prayers and authority. Is it really worth it? Just pray for them once and for all, let it go, and then leave it between them and God. At that point, it is no longer any of your business.

So, I have learned to look past the person and just blame whatever they did or are doing to me on the devil himself because that is truly the reality of it. God's word said that **the devil had come to kill, steal, and destroy**, not Jack, Jane, or Joe. It is just the devil operating through them to get to you. If you can convert your thinking in this manner, you will win the forgiveness battle every time. Forgiving will truly become very easy to do once you do not fall into this trap and you comprehend who your true enemy is; it is the devil, not them. The other person who is sinning against you is also a victim. Because the devil is controlling and deceiving them and, in return, will go back and collect their bad seed harvest from them that they planted when they sinned against you. Do not create your own negative seed time and harvest over them!

I have even learned to enjoy forgiving people because that really infuriates the devil. As the saying goes, "The enemy of my enemy is my friend."[7] I really enjoy destroying his battle plan against me. What is even more enjoyable is that I outsmarted him and did not fall for his trick. I realized it was him

---

7   Wikipedia Contributors, "The Enemy of My Enemy Is My Friend," in *Wikipedia, The Free Encyclopedia,* June 15, 2024, https://en.wikipedia.org/w/index.php?title=The_enemy_of_my_enemy_is_my_friend&oldid=1229288595.

trying to harm me, not them. They may have been the gun that the devil used, but we know guns do not kill; the perpetrator does. More importantly, I avoided my bad seed time and harvest. Even if their offense cost me something, I will let it go because the devil will have to give me back seven times what he stole from me if I do not fall for this unforgiveness trap.

So, really, it is the best return on investment that you could ever hope for, especially when you could only dream for sevenfold in the natural. Also, you receive a spiritual blessing with peace in your heart and mind. You just forgive them and command the devil to give back what he stole from you sevenfold in the name of Jesus by using your authority over him. This is God's spiritual law and government from His word, and He must return it sevenfold. You will come to understand that forgiveness does become something easy to do with a little practice, especially when you see it is the devil that is your true enemy, not them… and not be naive and fall for his trap.

It is sad to say, but the worst portrayal of unforgiveness is in the Kingdom of God. There are more dead bodies buried on this earth through fights and wars over religion than any other cause. At least they used religion as an excuse. I am going to stay neutral for a moment. What is interesting to me is that most religions are based on love. So, why is it that there is more unforgiveness within them? There has to be some kind of breakdown here.

There are either religions that are not based on love as they portray or the people are not operating in what that religion portrays. True love is best portrayed through forgiveness. So how could anybody, regardless of their beliefs, hate, resent, despise, or want to harm you?

Here is my conclusion. Many religions are based on God, and even though we have different views, we all have one thing in common. We all have a common and combined enemy, and that is the devil. He is the same devil that is here to **kill, steal, and destroy**. He does it through unforgiveness, which creates division. It does not matter to him how he does it as long as he can create division. *"A house divided within in itself will not stand"* (Matthew 12:25 NKJV). Be it liberal versus conservative, Protestant versus Catholic, one race over another, Cowboy versus Jet fan, one religion versus another. All he has to do is create unforgiveness and division, and he can have a steady stream of *killing, stealing, and destroying*—not just physically, but more importantly, spiritually.

Regardless, as children of God, we just know that we must forgive unconditionally just like God forgives us unconditionally. It truly is easy to do if you have revelation knowledge of the fourth simple truth, which is **forgiveness**, and the devil is our true enemy, not our fellow man that he may be working through at the time.

CHAPTER 9

The Five Simple Truths—Fifth... Love

Everything we have discussed previously works in conjunction with and through love. Everything that God has done for us is because of love. The subject of love was so important that it was the only commandment that Jesus left us to live by.

> *And thou shalt love the Lord thy God with all thy heart, and with all thy soul, and with all thy mind, and with all thy strength: this is the first commandment. And the second is like, namely this, Thou shalt love thy neighbor as thyself. There is none other commandment greater than these.*
>
> — Mark 12:30–31 (KJV)

If we are operating in love, we will not end up in sin in any other category. This new commandment of love would replace the old law that was given with the Ten Commandments and the curses that applied to it. Since the death, burial, and resurrection of the Lord Jesus Christ, we no longer live under the old law. Jesus paid for all of that. Jesus replaced the old law with a single new commandment, the **commandment of love**. How can we receive love from the Father, and it not flow through us? God does not just have love; he is love. So, if God is love and lives in us, then He wants to share it with the world through us. Love also works in conjunction with **seed time** and **harvest** and **forgiveness**.

Remember God's funnel discussed earlier? Do you want to receive a harvest of love? Then, plant a seed of love to each and every person you encounter. So, every person you come in contact with, you have an opportunity to sow a seed of love and get an abundant harvest of love in return. That does not always mean that your harvest of love will come back from that particular person, but it will still come back to you from somewhere; it is a spiritual law.

Love can come in many forms. In many cases, the act of love is a non-action. Think of a nasty, mean, vile person who is verbally attacking or talking about you or someone who cuts you off in traffic. Sometimes, the very act of love is just not giving them back what they gave you. Then, you just forgive them, whether they ask for it or not, as discussed earlier in the truth of forgiveness chapter.

They will receive their own harvest based on their actions by the seed they just planted. Regardless, you do not have to let them interfere with your harvest. I am about to write something that might be a little hard to digest...

Depression can be caused by many things. It can be inherited, caused by a chemical imbalance in our brains, or brought on by life situations. Whatever the cause, depression is the essence of the height of self-centeredness, which is the opposite of love. In this situation, this means when one is depressed, their only thoughts are how they feel, what they do not have, or what is happening to them in their life.

It is really sad to see cases where depression is brought on by something negative that happens to a loved one. The devil gets to try and destroy two lives at the same time. All these situations may be very well justified and a residual of what we are going through or something from our past that just would not let us go, or we do not want to let go. Unfortunately, the devil will take full opportunity to use our past to destroy our future.

I am definitely not making light of people who suffer from clinical depression. It is a horrible thing. It is an atrocious disease like cancer or any other thing that the devil would put on us. We must know that Jesus took stripes on His back to pay for our healing from depression, the same as He did for cancer. Whatever the cause, in this situation, love is proven to be a highly effective weapon against it.

When someone is in this situation, and even just operating in the natural realm, if they will only go find someone else to encourage, you will be encouraging yourself in the process. Operating in love for someone else and encouraging them releases endorphins in our brains that cure us of the very element we are fighting when we are encouraging and lifting somebody else up and putting them first before ourselves.

When I say by operating in love and encouraging someone else, that means not going and dumping all your problems on them, that would just turn into misery loves company. That would be the devil's dream come true. However, if we are operating in pure love by encouraging the other person, we are encouraging our own spirit in the process. I like to call it...

preaching myself happy. This operates in the spiritual law of seed time and harvest. As the saying goes, love never fails.

Depression is also part of the victim mentality, which is a trap from the devil to defeat us. Depression is also a byproduct of unbelief. When you are operating in faith (absence of unbelief), you have no reason to be depressed. Because if you are operating in faith, you know who you are in Christ and all that He has done for you. Along with all that is available to you as a child of God to bring you the joy and peace in your heart that you need and God desires you to have. No matter what first brought on the depression.

Now, let's talk about the most important love of all. The fact that God loves us with an agape type of love that we cannot even comprehend nor offer in the flesh. Think for a moment of the person you would say that you loved the most on this earth. Now, imagine loving them a hundred times more than that. That is the kind of love God has for you. You truly are God's pride and joy, and He has your picture in His wallet… LOL.

> *Behold, I have indelibly imprinted (tattooed a picture of) you on the palm of each of My hands; [O Zion] your walls are continually before me.*
>
> — Isaiah 49:16 (AMPC)

It is so important that we understand and have revelation knowledge of the magnitude of the love that God has for us. We discussed earlier that getting our prayers answered is not having more faith; that was a gift from God. Your born-again spirit has the **faith** of God. It is our unbelief that is keeping the word of God working for us. However, when you comprehend how much God loves you, you have confidence knowing that He does not want all the negative things that are happening in your life or the sickness and diseases that the devil is trying to put on you. He wants you to fulfill your marvelous destiny that He has planned for your life.

Now, think about the person that came to your mind when I asked you who you loved the most on this earth. Now, think about what you would do for this person if they would **allow** you and what kind of life you would like them to have.

> *When I think of the wisdom and scope of his plan, I fall down on my knees and pray to the Father of all the great family of God—some of them already in heaven and some down here on earth—that out of his glorious, unlimited resources he will give you the mighty inner strengthening of his Holy Spirit. And I pray that Christ will be more and more at home in your hearts, living within you as you trust in him. May your roots go down deep into the soil of God's marvelous love; and may you be able to feel and understand, as all God's children should, how long, how wide, how deep, and how high his love really is; and to experience this love for yourselves, though it is so great that you will never see the end of it or fully know or understand it. And so at last you will be filled up with God himself.*
>
> — Ephesians 3:14–19 (TLB)

That is why I have this prayer of Ephesians, which you can pray for yourself at the end of this book. Because when you have revelation knowledge of who you are in Christ and how much He loves you, the unbelief of God not honoring His word and His promises are eradicated. When you truly have revelation knowledge of how much God loves you, you will see that He wants you to receive His promises and provision even more than you do.

So, what am I saying? The *Five Simple Truths* are way more informational and impactful than you could imagine. They are condensed summaries of an enormous amount of revelation knowledge from God's word. Almost every sentence in this book came from some form of revelation knowledge of God's word. I put it in the shortest form possible so it will be easy to learn and easy to execute. With these *Five Simple Truths*, you can have an extremely successful Christian life and a walk with God without making it extremely complex. You can build your weapons of warfare against the devil while living in power, success, authority, and purpose and be complete in every area of your life… be it healing: physically, mentally, spiritually, or financially. At the same time, that is what is really cool about God and the Bible. Also, it can be deeply philosophical—theology in all of its comprehensive complexity, with prophecy, code-breaking, and history. However, that just depends on you, your personality, your goals, and God's plan for your life.

So, you can have it simple with all its power or extremely complex. That is up to you! However, with these *Five Simple Truths*, you can destroy the kingdom of darkness, avert the devil's attacks against you and be successful. Also, this gives you the platform and freedom to pursue and achieve the meaning of life that God has set before you. We could also dive into the baptism of the Holy Spirit and the nine gifts of the Holy Spirit, but that is another book in itself. Again, that is not complicated either. I just believe if we focus on these *Five Simple Truths*, God will lead us into these other things through the process of renewing our minds, which will give us even more power and ability to walk out His destiny for our life. Also, these are effective tools for the father on this earth while we are here.

So, at some point in your spiritual growth, I suggest that you research this topic for yourself, and the Holy Spirit will lead you to it. He said that *if we seek Him with our whole heart, we will find Him* (Jeremiah 29:13). The baptism of the Holy Spirit is a subject that is too big for this book, and it deserves its own book… LOL. But seriously… if you would like to know more about the baptism of the Holy Spirit, a good place to start is to read Acts 8:12–17 (ASV)…

> *But when they believed Philip preaching good tidings concerning the kingdom of God and the name of Jesus Christ, they were baptized, both men and women. And Simon also himself believed: and being baptized, he continued with Philip; and beholding signs and great miracles wrought, he was amazed. Now when the apostles that were at Jerusalem heard that Samaria had received the word of God, they sent unto them Peter and John: who, when they were come down, prayed for them, that they might receive the Holy Spirit: for as yet it was fallen upon none of them: only they had been baptized into the name of the Lord Jesus. Then laid they their hands on them, and they received the Holy Spirit.*

Now that we have the *Five Simple Truths*, which is the devil's greatest fear come true, he is going to do everything he can to steal them from you. Because if he cannot, he does not stand a chance in hell against you. What he is coming for is your **faith** and **authority**! Your faith in and on God's word, His promises, and everything that Jesus paid for you by His death, burial, and resurrection.

In the next few chapters, the focus is on exposing some of the devil's weapons so that we can protect our *Five Simple Truths* from the deceptive lies of the devil. We will expose the devil's lies and his vulnerabilities and protect our *Five Simple Truths* with revelation knowledge. In order to fulfill the meaning of our lives, we have to operate in the *Five Simple Truths*. We cannot operate in the *Five Simple Truths* if we do not have the revelation knowledge of how to protect those truths so that we can operate in them.

CHAPTER 10

The Devil's Four Greatest Weapons

Now that we have covered the *Five Simple Truths*, it is imperative that we cover the four biggest weapons the devil uses to destroy them. Because if you do not have the knowledge and the weapons to protect your *Five Simple Truths*, he will endeavor to rob them from you in order to defeat you. Also, if you do not have the revelation knowledge of these weapons, he can and will defeat you. More importantly, he cannot if you have renewed your mind on a strong foundation of revelation knowledge of these four weapons and how to guard against them.

One and two of these weapons are fear and worry and are the strongest, most used weapons the devil has and uses them against us to defeat us. The third is unbelief. Next, the fourth is deceiving you to keep you from finding out who you are in Christ with the authority given to you by and in the name of Jesus.

These are very clever tactics that the devil uses against us because he can work them from different directions and end up in the same place. He can push fear and worry to create unbelief about God's promises in our hearts, or fear and worry can be the byproduct of unbelief within us about God's word.

It is unbelief that nullifies our faith, and fear and worry are a byproduct of unbelief. He can use fear and worry to create unbelief. Fear and worry are actually a demonic spirit raging in warfare in our minds. It is a demon on your shoulder, so to speak, whispering in your ear.

> *Behold, I have given you authority to tread upon serpents and scorpions, and over all the power of the enemy: and nothing shall in any wise hurt you.*
>
> — Luke 10:19 (ASV)

Jesus is not talking about literal serpents and scorpions; He is talking about demons and evil spirits. Jesus has given you complete authority to rebuke and bind them away from you in the name of Jesus. When you are attacked with fear and worry in your mind, you must take authority (use your words) over them in the name of Jesus and command them to leave. Fear and worry will not leave if you do not tell them to in the name of Jesus. When you understand that fear and worry are actually literal demons, your mind will change concerning them.

What if you could physically see that demon sitting on your shoulder? Would you let him just sit there and run his big, nasty, ugly mouth? Or would you get a broom and chase that sucker out of your house, down the street, or even to the next state… LOL. Fear and worry will destroy you and everything you try to do and completely disarm everything God's word and the *Five Simple Truths* provide you.

Here in the book of Mark is an example of Jesus encouraging Jairus with two very important contrasting truths working together. Jesus was telling him to "Fear not, only believe." Remember, you cannot do both at the same time.

> *And there cometh one of the rulers of the synagogue, Jairus by name; and seeing him, he falleth at his feet, and beseecheth him much, saying, "My little daughter is at the point of death: I pray thee, that thou come and lay thy hands on her, that she may be made whole, and live." And he went with him; and a great multitude followed him, and they thronged him.*
>
> *While he yet spake, they come from the ruler of the synagogue's house, saying, "Thy daughter is dead: why troublest thou the Teacher any further?"*
>
> *But Jesus, not heeding the word spoken, saith unto the ruler of the synagogue, "Fear not, only believe." And he suffered no man to follow with him, save Peter, and James, and John the brother of James. And they come to the house of the ruler of the synagogue; and he beholdeth a tumult, and many weeping and wailing greatly. And when he was entered in, he saith unto them, "Why make ye a tumult, and weep? the child is not dead, but sleepeth."*
>
> *And they laughed him to scorn. But he, having put them all forth, taketh the father of the child and her mother and them that were with him, and goeth in where the child was. And taking the child by the hand, he saith unto her, "Talitha cumi;" which is, being interpreted, "Damsel, I say unto thee, Arise."*

> *And straightway the damsel rose up, and walked; for she was twelve years old. And they were amazed straightway with a great amazement.*
>
> — Mark 5:22–24, 35–42 (ASV)

What was the most important thing to observe from this scripture? It is what Jesus' response to Jairus was; He said, *"Fear not, only believe."* Then Jesus blurted this out before Jairus even had a chance to respond because He was trying to get him not to have fear so that it would not create any unbelief. When Jesus arrived there, He removed everyone that was there and only took in the child's parents and His disciples. This was to get rid of all the unbelief from anywhere around Jairus, his wife, and the situation. Jesus told him to *"Fear not, only believe"* (Mark 5:36 ASV).

Remember, our faith is perfect, and it lives in our spirits where God lives within us. We are feeding on God's word to remove unbelief from our souls and minds where the devil is raging war on us about the things that we are standing on our faith for from God's word and His promises. As we do this, our spirits start taking control like it is supposed to and start getting our minds and emotions lined back up to God's word and His promises.

Like I said earlier, faith is simple; man has only made it complicated. Fear and worry will make everything you fear and worry about come true. This is part of seed time and harvest. Remember the story of Job we talked about? Also, remember, even Job had a **"hedge of protection"** (Job 1:10 AMP) at one time, and the devil could not touch him until Job (not God) lowered it with his **seed time and harvest** of fear and worry.

When the seeds of Job's words of fear, worry, and lack of faith in God's word and His promises were planted, it opened the door for the devil. Then look at what Job received in return for it, his **seed time and harvest**. Do you want to receive what Job received? Then, just do what Job did and live in fear and worry.

This **hedge of protection** is what I also mentioned earlier and is called *"building and fortifying your walls and arsenal of protection"* before the enemy shows up at your gates. That has to be up and ready before, not during, or after the devil shows up to **kill, steal, and destroy**. In fact, I believe that fear and worry will drop this wall of protection faster than even sin will.

Fear and worry are actually sins. Furthermore, even in a sinful situation, I am still robed in the righteousness of Christ and operate in His righteousness and authority, not my own, as discussed earlier. However, fear and worry are another ball game. I am not going to sugarcoat it because it is so vital that you comprehend that it is just an inevitable spiritual law and fact, *whatsoever you sow, that shall you also reap* (Galatians 6:7). Even in the natural, if you plant a seed of corn, what is going to come out of the ground? Corn! So, do not sow the seeds of fear and worry from the start.

Fear and worry completely destroy **faith** because it manifests as unbelief. If we truly trusted God and had **faith** in His word, we would have no reason to be afraid, depressed, or worried. If we truly had **faith** and put God's word in first place, which is applying God's word correctly, there would never be a reason to have any fear or worry.

Faith is the only thing that keeps the things that you fear and worry about from coming to pass or things that you are praying for to come to pass. I have learned as long as I am operating in and under the *Five Simple Truths*, praying the Psalm 91 prayer over my family and me, and having a personal relationship with God.

I live inside this **hedge of protection** around me, and I can feel it tangibly. It is as tangible as solid ground under my feet or a roof over my head during a storm. When it is there, despite being a worry wart by nature, I am fearless with and against anything in front of me. However, it is there only because I am operating in the Kingdom of God by following the *Five Simple Truths*. I am human also; I get busy in life sometimes and start getting a little lax on my prayer and fellowship time with God and His word like I know I should do. Then, before I know it, fear and worry start slowly creeping in until it turns into full-blown fear, worry, and stress.

Fear and worry have become my **warning signal** that I am allowing my hedge of protection to start creeping down like Job did. It is like sirens and flashing lights that start going off inside me. Then I go running back to God's arms of protection as fast as I can by building myself (my wall of protection) back up with the word of God and reminding myself of who I am in Christ.

How do I know my hedge of protection is back up in place? When fear and worry are gone! It truly is just ridiculously simple. When operating in the Kingdom of God through **faith**, you can face this life without fear and worry and be as bold as a lion in the face of anything this world could possibly throw at you. How do I know this? Because I know what it says in Romans 8:28 and how it applies to me.

So, no matter what happens, when it is all over, I will still be standing, and I know I will be victorious even if I did go through some type of storm or crisis that the devil tried to put in my life. I may even have ended up with a few bruises and a couple of flesh wounds from it. However, when it is all over, I will still be standing and have victory over it, and will be stronger and more prosperous than before it happened. Glory to God! When the devil creates a storm in my life, somewhere about the halfway point, I actually start getting a little excited because I know when it is all over, I am going to end up way better than I was before.

Reflecting back, it seems like every major blessing or accomplishment in my life had a storm that preluded it. The storm that the devil was throwing at me was trying to prevent me from receiving something glorious that God desired to give or help me accomplish something major in my life. I know it sounds crazy, but again, I get a little excited when the devil tries to flex his muscles. I know something awesome is on its way, and as long as I do not fall for the fear and worry trap, I will receive it! When you truly can see it like this, you have no reason to fear or worry.

> *And we know that all things work together for good to them that love God, to them who are the called according to his purpose.*
>
> — Romans 8:28 (KJV)

God is not saying the storms that the devil attacks us with are **good**. Instead, what God is saying is that He will turn them out for our good despite what the devil intended. If we are doing our best to live in His will and destiny, operate in the kingdom of God with the *Five Simple Truths* by faith with our authority, and take control of the emotions of fear and worry, God can then and will turn them out for our good.

So, I do not tolerate fear or worry for any length of time in my life. I take authority over fear and worry in the name of Jesus, and I feed on God's word and His promises to remove unbelief from my **faith** that was attacked by fear and worry. The devil is a little creative sometimes and tries to put just a little on me, maybe just enough that I would tolerate it. However, fear and worry are a fire that will get out of control and turn into a forest fire if you do not put it out immediately. And I do so immediately! So, when fear and worry come, even the tiniest hint of it, you eradicate it immediately while it is still small and manageable through praise and worship over the promises of God in His word. However, even if we get hit suddenly with a large dose of the devil's fear and worry, we still have ways to manage it so that we will get to it in a minute.

I hate to put this so brutally honest, but your only alternative is not to do it and not only allow but cause everything you fear and worry about coming into reality in your life like Job did. I promise you that the devil will come to reap your seed time and harvest of the things you have fear and worry about.

Also, keep in mind that the devil is nothing but a bully. He only goes after the fearful and the weak. As the old saying goes, "Project strength to avoid conflict."[8] The devil cannot read our minds, but he can see the glow of our confidence beaming out of our spirits (life). Because by knowing who we are in Christ, we are free of fear and worry. When the devil sees the strength and confidence that we have from the life of God that lives

---

8   Bohdi, February 17, 2016.

within us… when we live a life free from fear and worry, he will just pass us on by for easier prey.

There is one more element to touch on when it comes to fear and worry because it is vitally important to understand so that you do not have to be ignorant of the devil's devices. The devil wars against us in our humanity in the natural realm. Fear and worry only operate in our emotions in the natural realm. Our born-again spirits are ten feet tall and bulletproof because of who we are in Christ and the life of God that lives within us. The devil would never take on a child of God in the spiritual realm. As a child of God, there is more power in our spiritual little fingers than the devil has in his whole kingdom because of who we are in Christ and the fact that we are robed in His righteousness and operate in His authority.

The devil does not have any authority; to have authority, he has to rob our authority with our words and use our authority against us. However, if we fall for his fear and worry trap and allow him to use seed time and harvest with our words against us just like he did with Job, then he can defeat us just like he did Job. He will only attack us in our weak humanity in the emotional realm.

Fear and worry are actually sins. Fear and worry must become as sinful and hideous to you as pedophilia. The only reason why I used the analogy of pedophilia is because I could not find anything worse on this planet than that, or I would have. That is because it is the most serious threat we face from the devil. I came across a teaching from Andrew Womack called *Harnessing Your Emotions*. Please look up this four-part teaching on YouTube, which you can watch for free. Without this teaching, I do not think I would have ever completely learned how to take complete control over my emotions or have the true understanding and importance of it—to have strong enough motivation to fight against it and complete control over fear and worry that is nothing but emotions.

That is the biggest destroyer of **faith** and the number one and two weapon by far that the devil uses against us. I think controlling your emotions is the most important thing to understand because that is the very first thing you must do when you face any battle, big or small. If you cannot control your emotions in a battle, which manifests in the flesh as fear and worry, which attaches unbelief to your **faith**, the battle is over in a split second. In sports terms, you are knocked out in the first second of the first round and completely eliminated. However, let me give you a simple little explanation that stuck with me from this teaching about harnessing your emotions and what I have used in any and every battle since.

If fear and worry are the biggest destroyers of faith (when we let our emotions take control over us), then we should use the exact opposite of that when faced with it in any battle. So, what would be the exact opposite of fear and worry? **PRAISE** and **WORSHIP**! Because it ushers in joy and peace, which is the opposite of fear and worry!

I have learned that the very second I am hit with anything that in the natural would make me have a reason to have any fear and worry, I should just start declaring and praising God about His word and His promises that promise me I will have victory over what the devil is trying to put on me! And I do not care who is around me! That does not mean if you are in a quiet public place that, you should make a scene and start singing, dancing, and praising God and screaming at the devil, taking authority over his demons of fear and worry. In those cases, I get to my feet immediately and start praising God out loud, professing His word and His promises, but as quietly as I can without making a scene as I am steadily heading to someplace where I don't have to worry about it.

God said we had to operate in love and forgiveness with our fellow man, but He did not say anything about that where the devil was concerned. I am headed to someplace where I can hit him with both barrels. As they say, there is a thing called holy anger. When I say the very second, I mean the very nanosecond when hit with something, I start praising God! It is like a bulletproof vest when the bullets start flying.

This is so vitally important to do, and I will explain why. As hard as it is for humans to control their emotions to start with, it is still a thousand times easier than trying to reign emotions back in once you let them get out of control in the first place. Even though controlling our emotions can be challenging, it is still completely up to us and our responsibility to do it. Most importantly, if we do not take control in the very beginning, it is going to take a spiritual giant to turn that situation around.

I guess that is kind of an oxymoron because if you are a spiritual giant, you will not allow the emotions to become out of control in the first place… Because you have enough revelation knowledge of God's word that if you do not, you will have already lost. The devil has you backed in the corner, but you are coming out swinging with the sword of the Spirit, which is the word of God and His promises. You have the chest plate of righteousness and the authority paid for by the Lord Jesus Christ. You have your shield of **faith** given by God to quench all the fiery darts of the devil who is trying to get unbelief attached to your **faith**.

> *Last of all I want to remind you that your strength must come from the Lord's mighty power within you. Put on all of God's armor so that you will be able to stand safe against all strategies and tricks of Satan. For we are not fighting against people made of flesh and blood, but against persons without bodies—the evil rulers of the unseen world, those mighty satanic beings and great evil princes of darkness who rule this world; and against huge numbers of wicked spirits in the spirit world. So use every piece of God's armor to resist the enemy whenever he attacks, and when it is all over, you will still be standing up. But to do this, you will need the strong belt of truth and the breastplate of God's approval. Wear shoes that are able to speed you on as you preach the Good News of peace with God. In every battle you will need faith as your shield to stop the fiery arrows aimed at you by Satan. And you will need the helmet of salvation and the sword of the Spirit—which is the Word of God.*
>
> — Ephesians 6:10–17 (TLB)

You must take control of your emotions and start praising and worshiping so that it ushers in joy and peace, and the unbelief will roll off you like water off of a duck's back. The devil is down for the count by a TKO. Also, in any battle situation, you are doing four things at the same time:

1. You are declaring the word of God and using it as a weapon against the devil.
2. You are praising God for the scriptures you are declaring over the situation.
3. You are operating in *seed time and harvest* with the words out of your mouth that you are declaring.
4. You are standing in faith on God's word and His promises that the words you are declaring will not come back void as God has promised.

However, before you misunderstand me about what I meant concerning a spiritual giant… It is just someone who simply understands their limitations and understands the simple fact that the biggest tool that the devil uses against us is fear and worry. Then, do not let fear and worry through your emotions get out of control from the onset. So, as soon as you can comprehend this, as simple as it is, and learn how to take control of your emotions from the very beginning, then I will consider you a spiritual giant. Because that is miles ahead of the average Christian, and it is very sad to have to say. The average person is a slave to their emotions.

Another way to look at fear and worry is the victim mentality. We have this almost uncontrollable emotional need in the flesh to feel sorry for ourselves in a bad situation and have someone to feel sorry for us if we are in pain or a crisis. The devil uses this weakness of the flesh with fear and worry to destroy us in every battle if we fall prey to this trap. However, if you can understand this simple truth, you will have enough pride in yourself and faith in God not to be tricked by the devil with such simplicity—by falling for the victim mentality and letting your emotions take control over you. This may be a hard truth, but in every situation, you must decide which one you want: do you want pity, fear, and worry, or do you want victory? You cannot have both. It will be a choice that only you can make in every situation. The choice you make will determine victory or defeat.

I could give you so many real-life testimonies where the devil has come against my family or me. I am sure you have also had cases in your life as well. I will just touch on one that I mentioned earlier because it is still the worst one I have ever faced. This testimony would take a book in itself to convey all that transpired before, during, and after and how awesome God is and what I learned through it. In fact, God validated everything He had taught me with the *Five Simple Truths* and His word and promises. It was when my son died and was dead for forty-three minutes at Keck Hospital in Los Angeles, California, but God raised him from the dead.

Where did my strength come from when I was outside his room when he was dead? And yet, I was dancing and singing and praising the Lord trusting God (taking control of my emotions) that what He promised me, in His word, He was able to perform. It did not come from my strength; everyone who knows me knows I am a worry wart by nature. I am living proof that being a worry wart does not disqualify you from being able to operate in the Kingdom of God with the *Five Simple Truths,* as well as controlling your emotions. Nor does it give you an excuse not to. You just have to renew your mind and find out who you are in Christ and what He paid for at the cross.

Once you understand that it is your choice, you can choose to go in either direction, and that is up to you. This is one thing that I learned from the experience of the battle that night that I never truly understood before. Nehemiah 8:10 (KJV) says, *"The joy of the Lord is our strength."* For the first time in my life, I experienced and understood what it really meant when it said, *"The joy of the Lord is your strength,"* which is *"joy unspeakable and full of glory."*

> *Whom having not seen, ye love; in whom, though now ye see him not, yet believing, ye rejoice with joy unspeakable and full of glory:*
>
> — 1 Peter 1:8 (KJV)

When the **cold blue** lights went off, I saw my son's eyes roll to the back of his head, and he collapsed like a wet noodle and died. I instantly jumped into action like I had been trained to do. I took control of my emotions, took authority over death, and commanded him to live in the name of Jesus. I started praising God like I had never praised God before in my life. I was truly just taking control of my emotions like I had been trained to do as an act of obedience. However, it turned into something I had never experienced before to that degree.

I may have started off in a mechanical act of faith by praising God to subvert fear and worry, that the devil was trying to put on me to kill my son and defeat me. Instead, in the process, I became so overwhelmed with the **joy of the Lord** that I cannot even explain it in words. I had never experienced such overwhelming joy in my life in the natural realm, and there are no words to describe it in the natural either. The joy of the Lord became my strength!

Say... if someone came up to you and told you that you just won the $200 million lottery, which would not have even come close to the joy I felt. I guess the closest way to describe what it felt like would be this: what if someone called you on the phone and told you that your child was dead? Then, forty-three minutes later, they called you back and said, sorry, we had the wrong number, and it was not your child. Think of the very moment when you heard those words and try to imagine the enormous joy, relief, and euphoria that would have the title waved over you and flooded your spirit. That was what it felt like to me!

I guess, in reality, that is what happened; the only difference was I experienced that joy before I received the call back forty-three minutes later explaining that it was not so. I had to put God's word in first place, and in return, God's word came in first place over what I saw in the natural realm. That is how faith 101 works. And that is when I knew the battle was won and my son would live despite what I saw in the natural realm. The true joy of the Lord and joy unspeakable and full of glory that I truly never understood or could have comprehended had come upon me and was the source of my strength in that battle. Even though he was still dead in the natural realm at the time. That joy of the Lord only came by controlling my emotions with praise and worship.

So, let me take just a moment to make sure you understand what I mean personally by **praise and worship**. I am not just saying... Praise the Lord, Hallelujah to the King of Kings, etc., alone like some kind of scripted chant I have to repeat. I am praising God from my heart for who I am in Christ, that His word cannot and will not come back void. I am reciting and repeating God's word and His promises back to Him and into the face of the devil from God's word that promises me I have victory over whatever I am facing at the moment (seed time and harvest). Also, I will recite decrees that I have already been standing on about the situation based on God's word that promises it (seed time and harvest). I am praising Him for everything that I can think of that I have learned from the *Five Simple Truths*. Then, I keep praising Him until the joy in me that comes from God is stronger than the fear and the worry and the emotions from which the devil is trying to put on me.

In a battle situation, it is hard to explain what it feels like to me personally. However, I will do my best to explain it from my perspective. I feel like I am in a battle between Heaven and hell, and I am standing in the gap in the middle. It is up to me to decide who I am going to yield my **faith** to in that battle. If I yield my **faith** and my emotions in the goodness and promises of God, then joy is the emotional byproduct, and I win the battle. However, if I yield my emotions to the devil and allow fear, worry, and the victim mentality to take over me, then the devil wins that battle. So, I have my part to play, and it will determine the outcome.

> *I call heaven and earth to record this day against you, that I have set before you life and death, blessing and cursing: therefore choose life, that both thou and thy seed may live:*
>
> — Deuteronomy 30:19 (KJV)

In this verse, God has given you the choice between blessing and cursing and life or death for both you and your seed. Plus, He even gave you the choice He hopes and wants you to make. He said, *"Choose life!"* Regardless, it is still your choice to make in every battle you face based on how you react to it and in whom and what you place your faith. You can choose life (victory) by yielding your trust and faith on God's word and promises through praise and worship, which manifest in the emotion of joy unspeakable and full of glory, and that is where you win the battle. Alternatively, you can yield to the devil by falling into the trap of fear, worry, and victim mentality and lose the battle. Your desire for victory has to be stronger than your emotional need in the flesh to receive pity or the victim mentality. Life and death are in the power of the tongue.

Here is the key, and I know I am being very redundant in this powerful truth, but if there is anything you take away from this book, God, I hope it is this… You cannot wait for the enemy to show up at your gates and then think you have time to prepare for a battle. If you are not prepared in advance so that you can take control of your emotions, you will lose. If you have not built up your military, arsenal, and strength and are not prepared for battle with a renewed mind from God's word and His promises, you will lose. If you have not done this before the enemy shows up, you have lost the war before it even began.

Emphatically, I know if I was not prepared for that battle in advance by feeding on God's word and His promises and knowing who I was in Christ and what He has promised me, my son would not be with us today! It would not have been God's fault; it would have been mine. He set before us the choice between life and death and even gave us the answer… choose life.

What happens if you do not prepare for a test in school? You are going to fail. What happens if an army is not prepared for war? They are going to lose. So, how can we think we cannot be prepared for an inevitable battle because we have an adversary and think we are going to win if we are not prepared in advance? What happens in the future when the enemy comes for one of your children or resources? Are you or will you be ready? Will you already be prepared for battle? In God's word, it says that *"your adversary, the devil, as a roaring lion, walketh about, seeking whom he may devour"* (1 Peter 5:8 KJV). In our defense, if we are prepared, we can devour him instead.

Last but not least, the fourth weapon the devil uses to destroy you is robbing you of your authority. The devil has no authority. He has to rob your authority from you through deception and use it against you with the words out of your mouth. I pray in the name of Jesus that you will receive complete revelation knowledge of who you are in Christ and the authority that He has given you over the entire kingdom of darkness.

You will not find anywhere in the gospel where God said He was going to do something about the devil on your behalf. He told you to do something about the devil, not Him, He said in James 4:7 (KJV), *"Resist the devil, and he would flee from you."* Who is he going to flee from? You! One of the definitions of flee means "to run from, as in terror."[9] The devil is absolutely terrorized by you because he knows the authority that you have even better than most Christians. If you could only see yourself

---

9   Kenneth E. Hagin, *The Believer's Authority*, 2nd edition (Faith Library Publications, 1986).

through the devil's eyes, you would see that he trembles in fear and terror before you, and he does not stand a chance against you if he cannot deceive you. However, you must renew your mind from the word of God and get revelation knowledge of the authority that you do have.

A weapon is useless to you if you do not know you have one or how to use it. When the devil comes across a Christian who does not have revelation knowledge of who they are in Christ or the authority that they have, the devil will steal their lunch and pop the bag when he is done… LOL.

We mentioned earlier about Holy anger. There are many instances in the Bible where God was angry. Even Jesus was angry and took a whip and drove out the money changers for defiling the temple. Your body is the temple of the Holy Spirit, and sin, sickness, and disease are a defiling of the temple of God! God gave us the ability to be angry for a reason. It was given as a weapon of warfare against our enemy, the devil, and the kingdom of darkness. In fact, until we get fire-spitting mad enough, we tend to tolerate the attacks of the enemy and take on the victim mentality instead, which is instant defeat. When the devil comes against us, we must pick up our weapons, the **shield of faith** and the **sword of the Spirit**, which is the word of God, and fight back like our lives depend upon it because it does. So, when the devil comes against you, get mad, pick up your sword, and slice him to pieces with the word of God until victory is won!

Remember, the devil is nothing but a bully. His main victims are deceived concerning their authority and are fearful and weak. However, when he comes across a Christian who knows their authority and exercises their authority, he will *flee from them as in terror.* The kingdom of darkness has no choice but to bow the knee and yield to the name of Jesus and the authority we have to use it on His behalf.

> *That at the name of Jesus every knee should bow, of things in heaven, and things in earth, and things under the earth;*
>
> — Philippians 2:10 (KJV)

Sickness and disease must bow, depression must bow, poverty must bow, fear and worry must bow etc. That is why we must speak directly to whatever the attack is from the enemy using the authority of the name of Jesus. That is why, in my son's case, I spoke directly to death, took authority over it, and commanded him to live in Jesus' name.

I know I have mainly used the word **battle** as a term for when the devil is attacking us like it is always some kind of major warfare. Except to me, everything the devil does against us, no matter how big or small, they are all demonic, and I have complete authority in the name of Jesus over any and all. Satan and sin are synonymous terms. If anything comes from the devil, I do not want anything to do with it… be it sin, sickness, poverty, depression, fear, division, worry, unforgiveness, or doubt and unbelief. We are fighting all of these things in some form.

These, to me, are all considered a battle because I do not want anything the devil would put on me or try to keep me from having what belongs to me through God's promises in His word. I treat all battles the same, large or small. If we let the small ones slip by, they will turn into larger battles, so it is best to destroy them when they are still small issues. If the devil comes against my family or me in any way, I am going to try to punch him back ten times harder than he ever punched me with God's word and His promises (scriptures). I accomplish this by using my authority over him that was purchased for me by the death, burial, and resurrection of the Lord Jesus Christ, and God has put His robe of righteousness on me.

Remember, the devil is nothing but a bully; you have to project strength to avoid conflict. I am going to use everything I have learned from God's word and these *Five Simple Truths* against him if he comes to my gates. Then I am not just going to hit him with both barrels. As the old saying goes, I am going to hit him with every barrel that I can get my hands on from God's word and His promises. I will blast the devil with every promise I have in God's word in and over the issue that I can think of right to his face.

This book is actually an example of that. The night he tried to kill my son, I decreed and prophesied (seed time and harvest) that he would regret the day he ever laid a hand on my child. That there would be so many people who would have their minds renewed and set free, delivered, and healed from his testimony. This book is me punching the devil back ten times harder than he punched me. I want to be his worst nightmare so he will be the bully that he is and just go look for weaker prey. Without exception, if he makes it through my gates, I will use these same *Five Simple Truths* and the word of God to destroy him on the battlefield… and the battlefield is in our minds.

CHAPTER 11

The Devil's Secret Weapon Word

Now, I would like to expose and dismantle the most horrible and defeating word in the human language for a child of God. The devil has used this one word to steal more from the body of Christ than any other word in history. And that is the word **IF**! Remember earlier, we discussed that the devil does not have to get us to disbelieve God's word; he only has to get us to question God's word. When you are praying about something and you insert the word **if** into your prayer, you have just destroyed your faith to receive and have poisoned your seed, and it is dead in the ground. It is **dead on arrival**, as they say.

Uncertainty and unbelief come from the word **if**. There are limited times we need to use the word **if** in prayer when we do not have a scripture and verse of a promise in God's words concerning it. For instance, we discussed earlier when we are following God's will for our lives and our personal destinies that are personal to us, and we do not have a scripture and verse for it. What really infuriates me is when I hear even preachers praying over somebody for something like healing, and they say, "If it is God's will," it takes everything within me not to go full-blown ballistic and make a scene.

When we are praying about something, we only have to judge who the author of it is by asking two simple questions. Will the situation kill, steal, and destroy, which is something the devil is the author of? Or will it bring life and life more abundantly that Jesus promised us and died for the right to provide it for us? If it is something that will kill, still, and destroy in any shape, form, or fashion, make no mistake about it; it is from the devil. God never brings negative things into our lives to teach us something or to build our character that way. We may have been deceived by the devil and have made some bad decisions that brought negative things into our lives, but that was not God putting them on us.

Let's stay on the topic of healing for a moment as an example. I do not care what the situation is; if you are sick in any form, it did not come from God, and it **is** God's will to heal you. The devil is the author of sickness and disease. Since the death, burial, and resurrection of the Lord Jesus Christ and as a New Testament child of God, there is never a case where sickness is going to be God's will. Therefore, you have to know and have that settled in your heart to receive healing because the devil will use the word **if** to steal it from you with doubt and unbelief.

This might be a hard truth… If you fall for the trap of the devil with the word **if**, the only chance you have of healing is to be in the presence of someone with the gift of healing provided by the Holy Spirit. They are listed and described in the book of Corinthians in the 13th chapter concerning the nine gifts of the Holy Spirit, with the gift of healing being one of them, and the Holy Spirit has to be operating that gift through that individual while they are praying for you and your faith still has its part to play also.

Even the individual's faith hindered Jesus in His own hometown when He wanted to heal them. The gift of healing is for the Body of Christ, not for the individual who actually possesses that gift. Even a person who may have the gift of healing given by the Holy Spirit has to receive healing just like the rest of us do, by their own faith. So, God's best and will for you is for you to receive your own healing through your own **faith** in God's word and His promises. This is by knowing who you are in Christ and all that He paid for by the stripes on His back. Knowing that He has already paid for your healing, and all you have to do is receive it by faith. It is not by not falling for the trap of the devil with the "if it is God's will" lie out of the pit of hell! Again, it is by knowing that it is God's will to heal you and then stand in faith on God's word and receive the healing that Jesus already paid for you by the stripes on His back.

I think these gifts are primarily for newly born-again Christians who have not had time to build their revelation knowledge on God's word. Because if a new Christian were diagnosed with stage 4 cancer, they would not have had time to build their own revelation knowledge of who they are in Christ yet. God has provisions for every one of His children. Again, it is not God's best for you to receive healing that way based on the gift operating through a believer with the gift of healing on your behalf.

I will give you an example of this and why it is not the best way for you to receive healing through a believer operating with the gift of healing. Standing on your own faith is the best way. Kathryn Kuhlman, back in the 70s, had a profound healing ministry and she operated in the gift of healings and miracles by the Holy Spirit, which were very prevalent in her ministry. She was putting the wheelchair companies out of business... LOL.

I listened to an interview with her from many years ago, in which she described something that really broke her heart. She said she found out later that a percentage of people who did receive healing by the working of the gift of the Holy Spirit in her ministry ended up losing their healing sometime after that. Because they received their healing based on somebody else's gift and faith, but when they returned home, they had no revelation knowledge of it for themselves. Then the devil came and stole their healing from them with lying symptoms and doubt and unbelief. Because as an individual, they did not have revelation knowledge of who they were in Christ and that healing did, in fact, belong to them. So, do you see how vitally important it is to know God's will when it comes to healing?

One may say that God said we would not live forever and that the human life span was from at least 80 to the age of 120... max. That is true, but who said you had to die from sickness and disease that came from the fall of man that the devil is the author of in order to die?

That is how it happens in most cases because of the lies of the devil with the "If it is God's will" garbage. There are graveyards full of people who died before their time. It was not God's will for them to die, but they fell for that "If it is God's will **trap** or had no prior knowledge or faith about healing. There are many examples of this in the Bible where a man would bring in his children, give them their blessing, then give up his spirit and go home to be with the Lord. Even Moses, at the age of 120, had perfect strength, health, and eyesight, yet when it was his time to go home to be with the Lord, he just laid down, gave up his spirit, and went home. At the age of 120, he even climbed up a mountain to die.

Do you think climbing up a mountain is something that a sick person at the point of death could do at the age of 120? I have seen cases even in my family when the elderly have had their bodies finally just wear out, and then they peacefully went home to be with the Lord. That is how it is supposed to be, not dying of cancer and many other horrible sickness, disease, and pain like this that the devil has put on us.

Kenneth E Hagin gave a perfect example of this with an elderly lady in his congregation who was 82 years old and was dying from terminal cancer and had very few weeks left to live.[10] The devil had convinced her that it was just her time to go home to be with the Lord, and she had given up. Brother Hagin encouraged her not to die like this and to let the Lord heal her. Afterward, if she still wanted to go home to be with the Lord, that was fine… LOL. Except, do not die like this, with a horrible, painful death of cancer. Then he helped her lift up her faith, and she received complete healing and lived to be 92 years old. During that ten-year period of time, she traveled all over the world. She finally was able to do the traveling and see all the wonderful things that she had wanted to do her whole life but never had the chance to. Through her testimony, many other elderly people received their healing (and still are

---

[10] Rev. Kenneth E. Hagin, *Healing Classics* (Faith Library Publications, 1985).

and you are hearing about it right now, many years later) by lifting their faith up to receive as well.

What do you think that outcome would have been if he gave her one of those "If it is God's will" garbage kind of prayers? What about the loss of those ten wonderful years and all the other older adults who would have never been able to receive their healing as well? Just that one prayer over one single person with the **IF** word would have let the devil have a booming crop of killing, stealing, and destroying.

Now apply this one situation compounded with everyone in the graveyard we just discussed. Then you get the magnitude of what this word **IF** does to a child of God and the Kingdom of God. So, emphatically just know that it is God's will to heal you, and never fall for the "If it is God's will" trap. Also, remember that goes for every promise that God gave you in His word! God's word is God's will!

In the next Chapter, I will give a condensed version of putting a lot of what we have been learning into a real battle situation. It is called *The Five-Step Battle Plan*. It is similar to the *Seven Steps to an Answered Prayer* that is included at the end of this book. It goes into more detail to be thorough and cover all bases. However, *The Five-Step Battle Plan* is for someone who is starting to comprehend who they are in Christ by building their revelation knowledge from God's word. They are only a page long. Everyone is capable of completely memorizing them.

I remember that as a young man in sales, I had to memorize word for word a three full-page sales presentation. I had to accomplish that in three days. I was astonished that I and pretty much everyone with me at that training class had no problem accomplishing that. It is just a reminder that our human nature is willing to do things like this for jobs or competition, etc. And yet, we do not use that same God-given capability to meditate to renew our minds, learn God's word, and get it down deep in our souls.

I am not promoting memorizing the full page of *The Five-Step Battle Plan*. However, it would be helpful to memorize the first sentence of each one. It would be kind of like an emergency plan so that you can be prepared for battle at a moment's notice. Humans do not think clearly in an emergency situation. Whatever you have built down inside you in your spirit will be what automatically surfaces whether you want it to or not. So, let *The Five-Step Battle Plan* be your emergency plan strategy. At the same time, you do not have to be in an emergency situation to use them. It is the same five steps based on *The Five Simple Truths* that allow your faith to operate in the supernatural realm, where miracles exist on a regular basis by standing on God's word. Remember, miracles are nothing other than God's word and His promises coming to life in the natural realm, in and through your **faith** in God's word and His promises.

CHAPTER 12

The Five-Step Battle Plan

1. Be well prepared for the battle in advance. Meditate on God's word and His promises until they become deeply rooted and embedded into your spirit. Pray Psalm 91 and Ephesians prayer at the end of this book over you and your family regularly to pre-build your hedge of protection. Then God's word and His promises will become instantaneously available from within your spirit to use as weapons in prayer against the devil's attack through seed time and harvest.
2. Instantly take control of your emotions! Subvert fear and worry with praise and worship by declaring those promises out loud with your words in the devil's face. Praise God for the promises from His word that you are standing on in this situation. At the temptation of Christ, in every single attack, His only response to the devil in every attempt was God's word (scripture). While you declare these scriptures, you

are simultaneously operating in seed time and harvest, which is a spiritual law.

3. Meditate on how much God loves you. He died to give all of this to you. He loves you and wants you to be even more victorious over this situation than you do.
4. Know in your heart that in God's word, He has already given you and paid for everything. The Bible, Old and New Testament, is God's **last Will and Testament** to you. Furthermore, just like a **Will**, it is given to you; it is a free gift by grace. It is not earned because you cannot earn it with good works. Everything has already been paid for by the Lord Jesus Christ at the cross. Except, it is our responsibility to receive it and bring it into our possession like a will.
5. Start and keep praising God for His word and the promises in His word that promise you that you have victory over this situation until fear and worry that produce unbelief have left you. That is how you know you can stop praising at that time when the fear and worry have left you. Once all unbelief has been removed from your **faith**, your **faith** will work productively the way God designed it to work and turn the situation around.

Miracles do not exist in the natural realm. You are operating in the spiritual realm in the Kingdom of God, where miracles do exist. You are a spirit being operating in the spiritual realm. Drawing down the promises in God's word that exist in the spiritual realm and receiving them in the natural realm, by and through **faith**. Keep in mind that we are operating through **seed time and harvest**. So, our victory may be instant, or it could be over time, depending on the issue. However, you stand on God's word, and you keep standing on God's word and praise Him for it until the victory is won!

CHAPTER 13

Redeemed from the Curse of the Law

I remember, as a young Christian, hearing a preacher teach on the 28th chapter of Deuteronomy. Boy, that was one exciting sermon as God was saying all the blessings that would come upon me. His word said I would be blessed in the city, and I would be blessed in the field. I would be blessed when I am coming and blessed when I am going, etc. I could not wait until I could get home, get my Bible out, and start studying Deuteronomy chapter 28. When I did, I started with verse 1 all the way to verse 13, and it was so exciting. Then I hit verse 14, and everything changed… LOL. From verse 14 all the way to the end of the chapter, verse 68, it talks about all the curses.

As a young Christian, I started avoiding the 28th chapter of Deuteronomy as much as I did with the story of Job, which we discussed earlier. Eventually, through revelation knowledge about the 28th chapter of Deuteronomy, as I received about the story of Job, everything changed as well.

> *You foolish Galatians! Who has bewitched you? Before your very eyes Jesus Christ was clearly portrayed as crucified. I would like to learn just one thing from you: Did you receive the Spirit by the works of the law, or*

by believing what you heard? Are you so foolish? After beginning by means of the Spirit, are you now trying to finish by means of the flesh? Have you experienced so much in vain—if it really was in vain? So again I ask, does God give you his Spirit and work miracles among you by the works of the law, or by your believing what you heard? So also Abraham "believed God, and it was credited to him as righteousness." Understand, then, that those who have faith are children of Abraham. Scripture foresaw that God would justify the Gentiles by faith, and announced the gospel in advance to Abraham: "All nations will be blessed through you." So those who rely on faith are blessed along with Abraham, the man of faith. For all who rely on the works of the law are under a curse, as it is written: "Cursed is everyone who does not continue to do everything written in the Book of the Law." Clearly no one who relies on the law is justified before God, because "the righteous will live by faith." The law is not based on faith; on the contrary, it says, "The person who does these things will live by them." "Christ redeemed us from the curse of the law" by becoming a curse for us, for it is written: "Cursed is everyone who is hung on a pole. He redeemed us in order that the blessing given to Abraham might come to the Gentiles through Christ Jesus, so that by faith we might receive the promise of the Spirit.

— Galatians 3:1–14 (NIV)

In the passage above, it says, *"I had been redeemed from the curse of the law,"* So now verses 14–68 are just as exciting to me because I get to see all the things I have been redeemed from, not just what I have been blessed with, according to verses 1–14.

Many will try to use the old law from the Old Testament to say God puts sickness on a child of God or allows sickness for the consequences of sin. This is a lie out of the pit of hell to deceive and destroy you. Remember, we discussed earlier in the *Five Simple Truths* under **love** about the old law having been replaced by the new commandment of love? Jesus redeemed us from the curse of this law, and we are under the new commandment of love. **Love** replaced the **law**.

This will hinder your faith in receiving from God because it will bombard you with unbelief, thinking that God allowed it to teach you something or that you deserved it. That is complete hogwash. Now, there are lifestyles of sin that we could persist in that can bring sickness upon us. For example, if you drink alcohol in excess like an alcoholic, you can eventually get cirrhosis of the liver, but God did not put that on you or allow it; you did. Additionally, the devil seized every opportunity that you gave him.

God has already provided everything for you. You have been given everything pertaining to life and godliness, and you have been redeemed from the curse of the law. Since the death, burial, and resurrection of the Lord Jesus Christ, you would not see any place where God or Jesus put sickness on anyone. Or anything else listed under the curse of the law because we have been redeemed from the curse of the law.

> *As His divine power has given to us all things that pertain to life and godliness, through the knowledge of Him who called us by glory and virtue.*
>
> — 2 Peter 1:3 (NKJV)

We have been given all things, and we receive them through the knowledge of Him.

> *Blessed be the God and Father of our Lord Jesus Christ, who hath [past tense] blessed us with all spiritual blessings in heavenly places in Christ:*
>
> — Ephesians 1:3 (KJV)

We have already been blessed with every spiritual blessing through Christ Jesus.

> *Christ redeemed us from the curse of the law by becoming a curse for us,*
>
> — Galatians 3:13 (NIV)

Jesus paid for this curse on our behalf at the cross. So, just know in your heart that you are redeemed from every curse of the law. He has provided every blessing you could even think of, imagine, or dare to ask for, far beyond your wildest dreams and prayers. Equally important, He has paid it all for you in advance, and it belongs to you as a child of God. He has given us instructions in His word on how to receive what we have already been given. We do not have to wait for him to provide. I am going to create a scene for you that will help you understand the gravity of this situation that Jesus paid for at the cross.

Let's say that you were there on Jesus' day of crucifixion. What if you were able to see with your own eyes and experienced the Lord Jesus Christ being whipped with special whips with metal claws on the end of it? They beat Him with that whip until they literally ripped all the flesh and meat off His back and exposed His ribs. Now, think if He was to look up at you afterward and tell you personally that He did this just for you so you could receive your healing *"by whose stripes ye were healed"* (1 Peter 2:24 KJV). Now, imagine what it would feel like to Him if you walked away and said, "I just do not have enough faith to believe that, or if it is God's will to do so."

At that moment, He realized He just had gone through the worst torture men had to offer on this earth for nothing. Can you imagine that it broke His heart beyond comprehension? What would you feel like in this situation if the roles were reversed? This case scenario is the reality for Him when we do not receive the healing He paid for.

I only wrote this so you could begin to comprehend and have revelation knowledge that Jesus wants you to receive your healing and salvation way more than even you want you want them. He loves you more than you can comprehend. He went through hell on earth to provide it for you. It breaks His heart beyond human understanding when we do not receive what He paid an enormous price for.

When you receive revelation knowledge of…

1. that God loves you more than you can comprehend.

2. the price that Jesus paid for you was far worse than you could imagine. Knowing this will help you to receive what He paid for.
3. knowing the cost that was paid to provide it because of how much He loves you!
4. having revelation knowledge that you have been redeemed from the curse of the law.
5. being able to stand on your **faith** by removing the devil's lies that would cause unbelief in God's word to be attached to your **faith**.

Then, you will know that it is God's will to heal you, and it will remove all the unbelief from your faith so that you can receive the healing and salvation He has so terribly paid the price for.

I mainly used healing as an example of how we have been redeemed from the curse of the law. However, it is the same truth with every blessing and curse. We have the deluxe package; we have all the blessings and we are redeemed from all the curses. Glory to God! It may be spiritually, mentally, physically, financially, or anything to do with our destiny that He has for our lives while we are on this earth… we have been provided with every spiritual blessing and have been redeemed from every curse of the law!

CHAPTER 14

Faith Destroying Misconceptions

Now, I would like to clear up three horrible misconceptions about our heavenly father and one of our origins. To keep you from having stumbling blocks in front of you, laid out by the devil to lie and deceive us and try and steal your *Five Simple Truths* from God's word.

This subject I could write a book alone, but I just want to dismantle four of the big ones. I will endeavor to keep this as brief as possible, yet effective enough to send these lies back to hell from where they came. We have covered some of this already. I just want to get them all together and touch on these last four and put the final nail in the devil's coffin with all his lies. Lies to try and steal our *Five Simple Truths*.

NUMBER ONE

God is not, I repeat, God is not the author of sickness, disease, world catastrophe, and human suffering.

When God designed man in the Garden of Eden, he was meant to live forever, and this earth was to be in perfect harmony with itself. God designed us and the planet to be heaven on earth.

He made man perfect, built in His image and His likeness. Man's spirit came from God's own spirit and was a part of Him, just like we are physically a part of our earthly parents and came from their DNA.

God said, *"Let us make man in our image, after our likeness"* (notice He said *"our,"* meaning God, Jesus, and the Holy Spirit) (Genesis 1:26 KJV). Does God (Jesus) have sickness and disease? No, and neither should you and me. We are children of God and have His DNA. Satan is the author and the source of all of this!

In the garden, when man failed, it corrupted our physical seed as well as this planet's by activating the curse. It says in God's word concerning the devil, *"your adversary, the devil, as a roaring lion, walketh about seeking whom he may devour"* (1 Peter 5:8 KJV). Also, in God's word, it says that **the devil has come to kill, steal, and destroy** (John 10:10)!

Here is a little revelation knowledge that you need to receive from this verse. It says that he walks around **as** a roaring lion, not that he **is** one, and it says he is seeking whom he **may** devour, which means we do not have to let him; the choice is ours. As a child of God, there is more power and authority in our little finger than satan has in his whole kingdom.

Following the *Five Simple Truths* from God's word and building up our armor in advance through meditating on God's word of who you are in Christ and the authority He gave us renders Him absolutely powerless against us. Then, concerning Jesus, *"I have come that they [you] may have life, and that they may have it more abundantly"* (John 10:10b NKJV). Can we truly have an abundant life if we are sick, broke, depressed, oppressed with addictions, and defeated? In the Word, it says, Jesus *"came to destroy the works of the devil"* (1 John 3:8 NIV).

If we follow Jesus through the first four gospels in the Bible of His earthly ministry, what do we see Him do more than anything else, bar None?

He healed the sick, cast out devils, and made the lame to walk and the blind to see.

> *And this woman, a daughter of Abraham (redeemed from the curse of the law) as she is, whom Satan has bound for eighteen long years, should she not have been released from this restraint on the Sabbath day?*
>
> — Luke 13:16 (NASB)

Who had her bound? Satan, not God. All sickness and disease are the works of the devil, **NOT GOD**! Also, notice that there was never a time when Jesus put sickness or disease on anybody. Jesus was operating on this earth by doing God's will. It was God's will to heal in every instant. There were sickness and disease that came from the curse in the Old Testament, but that has been done away with since the death, burial, and resurrection of the Lord Jesus Christ has redeemed us from the curse of the law.

NUMBER TWO

Now, about world catastrophes.

At the fall of man, it corrupted not only the seed of man but also the planet and its atmosphere. If you read the story in the

Bible, when Jesus and the disciples were in a boat going across the Sea of Galilee, a great storm arose, and the disciples were fearful and woke Jesus up (He was not fearful; He was asleep, LOL.) and asked, *"Master, careith not that we perish?"*

> *And the same day, when the even was come, he saith unto them, Let us pass over unto the other side. And when they had sent away the multitude, they took him even as he was in the ship. And there were also with him other little ships. And there arose a great storm of wind, and the waves beat into the ship, so that it was now full. And he was in the hinder part of the ship, asleep on a pillow: and they awake him, and say unto him, Master, carest thou not that we perish? And he arose, and rebuked the wind, and said unto the sea, Peace, be still. And the wind ceased, and there was a great calm And he said unto them, Why are ye so fearful? how is it that ye have no faith?*
>
> — Mark 4:35–40 (KJV)

Picture this scene in your mind... Jesus arose, rebuked the storm, and then scolded them for their lack of faith. Jesus would not and could not do anything against something God was doing! He would not rebuke Himself for doing something wrong that needed rebuking.

A little side note, off topic about this verse. Why would Jesus scold them for their lack of faith concerning the storm if they could not have done something about that storm themselves? I will not go into all the details at this moment, but I have used the word of God and my authority over the weather in the name of Jesus more than once. I get fire-spitting mad when I read things like on an insurance policy where it says about an accident or a bad weather event, and they call it "An act of God!" It is "An act of the devil," and people blame God for it!

NUMBER THREE

Now, let's tackle human suffering.

I will keep this one super brief because anyone between a short-order cook and a rocket scientist can see this one. Look at all the countries that have high poverty and starvation rates. Those countries have enough resources that can make every citizen rich. It is man being controlled by the devil that exerts tyranny over their citizens to enrich themselves and deprive their citizens of what is available to them. As a child of the devil, they do the works of the devil. Remember, it says that **the devil came to kill, steal, and destroy** (John 10:10)!

Now look at murder, assault, rape, human trafficking, child and spouse abuse, and government ternary etc. Is that God? Are these performed by a child of God doing God's will? Or is it the devil working through the blind, brainwashed, deceived children of the devil doing his will? So, let's finish this off and clear these three questions up with just a little common sense.

If God is our father, and He is, what father would do this to his children? We would not, and neither would He! Satan is the author of all of this and then tries to convince the world it is God to cover his own evil and turn us against God! Classic cases of creating evil divert the blame to discredit somebody else!

It burns me up inside when even a child of God says that God brought something hurtful in their lives to "teach them something" or "I don't know why God is putting more on me than I can stand." I have even heard preachers use Romans 8:28 to say something so misleading... *"And we know that in all things God works for the good of those who love him, who have been called according to his purpose"* (NIV). That verse means just the opposite of how they used the verse. If you love God and are called according to His purpose, even if satan tries to bring things into your life to destroy you, God can turn them for your good if you operate in faith.

We can stand on God's word and His promises, turn it around for the glory of God and for ourselves and spit in the devil's eye in the process. A child can learn by putting his hand in a fire and it will burn them. However, would you put your child's hand in a fire to teach them? **NO WAY!** You would not, and neither would God. God's will is the same as yours... to try and direct and teach them with your words to keep these things from happening just like God does through His word in His word. Additionally, God gives us His Holy Spirit within us to lead us away from these dangers.

If you are in fellowship with Him and listening to Him by training your spirit to hear His voice... then when something negative comes or happens in your life, it is the devil trying to **kill, steal, and destroy,** and is not from God who sent Jesus so that we can *"have life and have it more abundantly"* (John 10:10 NKJV). Yes, we do learn from these things, but it was not God's will for you to learn them that way. That is just the devil trying to deceive you!

NUMBER FOUR

Last but not least, Creation versus Evolution.

This is not to get into a scientific debate but only for the purpose of not having a stumbling block between us and our personal relationship with our heavenly father. While going through years of education (indoctrination) that teaches evolution, it is almost impossible for many not to believe in evolution. Some places, you would be labeled as a fool and an idiot if you dared to think otherwise.

This belief is controlled by indoctrination and peer pressure (cancel culture). You keep hearing, "This is proved by science, this is proved by science," blah blah blah…. Our brain is like a computer, so whatever data you put in it is the only data you are going to get out. This is part of that biased mindset discussed earlier that controls us, and we do not even realize it.

If you are only taught (constant bombarding with indoctrination) on one side of any subject, that is the only part of the subject you will and can believe. Neither the creationists nor the scientists were around when it all happened. Everything put forth on both sides is a projection of their beliefs. Most of the things that scientists base everything on is carbon dating. But by their own admission, they agree that the only thing that would change carbon dating is if the object was underwater for an extended period of time (the flood). If that was so, it nullifies the ability to carbon date with any accuracy at all. Also, it is proven by scientists, based on rock formation and earth erosion and elements within the rocks and structures, that some large water event did indeed happen.[11] All agree that this happened and was caused during the flood based on Genesis's historical record and science.

So, science itself contradicts itself in two different directions because that would dramatically affect carbon dating and make it fallible. Also, the very tooth they originally found, they said it proved we came from monkeys, but many years later, with updated equipment, it turned out to belong to a pig.[12] Did they change all the science on which they based that discovery? No, they did not. So, that is not science. That is theory projected as truth and dares you to think otherwise.

However, the same goes for creation. There are geological discoveries that back up what we believe but still fall shy of infallible proof, just like the Evolution Theory. At least they still call it the Evolution Theory even though they projected it as fact and demanded you to take it as such. Still, there are areas where both could be partially correct and wrong in their hypothesis.

It says in God's word that a day and a thousand years are the same as unto the Lord (2 Peter 3:8). God is not limited by space or time. So, were those seven days of creation actually seven days known to man? Most theologians believe that, and that is what I believe as well. I am not an educated theologian to argue that point in either direction. Also, I take into account that in Genesis chapter 1:28, God said to *replenish the earth.*

---

11 "Startling Evidence for Noah's Flood," Answers in Genesis, 2024, https://answersingenesis.org/geology/grand-canyon-facts/startling-evidence-for-noahs-flood/.

12 Ibid.

Then, if He was *replenishing the earth,*" what was He replenishing it from, and for how long of a time period?

I do not have all the answers, but here is what I am saying. There are Christian creation scientists just like there are Atheist evolution scientists. Neither were on this earth as eyewitnesses for infallible proof of what they believe. Both sides say they are right, and the other side is wrong. However, the actual reality is that both fall short of infallible proof, **both take faith to believe in**. So, it is the individual's choice of where they want to place their faith in, man or in God.

Science says miracles do not exist, but they are proven wrong every day. So, they just bury their heads in the sand and pretend it never happened. Based on science, my son is supposed to be dead or, at best, a brain-dead vegetable, but the science was wrong. Again, science was proven fallible because supernatural spiritual law supersedes natural law in the natural realm.

In this case, if his mother and I had put our faith, hope, and belief in science instead of faith in and on God's word and promises, he would not be with us today. What I am saying is that they keep saying that science is infallible, and you have to believe whatever science says because they are never wrong.

Science told the world that if they received the vaccination, they would not get COVID-19 or be able to spread it. How did that turn out? Again, science was proven wrong. They want us to gamble our whole life and our eternity, be it Heaven or Hell, based on science that is proven wrong all the time instead of faith.

How we spend our lives and where we live for eternity is way too important and detrimental to put our lives in the hands of scientists who are proven wrong all the time. Do you think there will be any scientists in Hell apologizing to you for being wrong? Let's set evolution and creation aside for just a moment, and let's just use our own God-given common sense.

Here is a scientific question for you: what is nothing plus nothing? The answer is nothing. How could you create anything without having something to start with? Science can do some pretty amazing things, but even science cannot make nothing out of nothing. God is that something!

So, both sides can bring all kinds of evidence to prove their theories, but both fall short of being infallible, other than God's word is infallible. They both take faith to believe. However, I will say the Bible has been proven scientifically right many times based on geological findings that back up what is recorded in the Bible. I do not have any unbelief in my mind or soul that God created this earth.

If you are like me, then this issue is solved. I have already done extensive research in both directions. I do believe in the Big Bang Theory. The Big Bang happened when God opened His mouth and spoke, *"Light be."* And it is still traveling at the speed of light at 670,616,629 mph. However, if you still have questions about it and want to know more, I suggest you look up Dr. Kent Hovind. He also has a YouTube channel under *Genesis Baptist Church*. He is a joy to watch, and he blows so many holes in the Evolution Theory it is ridiculous; he can spit them out like a machine gun… LOL. He has specific teachings about Creation versus Evolution Theory from which you can research. From my understanding, he even has an exhibition park on 146 acres somewhere.

Also, Dr. Frank Turek has a book called *I Don't Have Faith to Be an Atheist*. You can also go on YouTube and watch videos of his as well. They blow evolution and an accidental Big Bang Theory out of the water. When you have all the information, it truly does take more faith to believe the Evolution Theory than it does creation.

CHAPTER 15

How to Be Led by the Spirit

Now, I will get back to where we started concerning *The Meaning of Life*, which is vitally important to understand and how to achieve it in our everyday life practically. God had a plan for our lives before He even put us in our mother's womb. He gave us our personalities, strengths, weaknesses, passions, intellect, and abilities, or even the lack thereof, for a specific purpose and journey to accomplish it. We can try to follow our path and try to achieve our goals that we think will fulfill us and bring us happiness and contentment. Still, even if we accomplish these things, we will still feel unfulfilled and empty. However, if we focus on asking Him in our prayer life to show us His will for our lives, He can lead us to a place that we could never imagine. Then that is if we will only trust Him and go where He leads us, just like He did Abraham. And yet, we have to trust (faith) God to do so.

Let's start by following God's will for our lives 101.

> *If you want to know what God wants you to do, ask him, and he will gladly tell you, for he is always ready to give a bountiful supply of wisdom to all who ask him; he will not resist it. But when you ask him,*

> *be sure that you really expect him to tell you [faith], for a doubtful mind will be as unsettled as a wave of the sea that is driven and tossed by the wind; and every decision you then make will be uncertain, as you first turn this way and then that. If you don't ask with faith, don't expect the Lord to give you any solid answer.*
>
> — James 1:5–8 (TLB)

The best way I can personally explain how to describe how to follow God's voice and His will for your life or any question you may have from God is this…

The number one way that God leads us is through His word. Some are literal in the word of God, like *"thou shall not kill"* (Exodus 20:13 KJV). It is God's will for you not to kill. It says in His word, *"Do not be unequally yoked together with unbelievers"* (2 Corinthians 6:14 NKJV). So, if you are wondering if it is God's will for you to marry a member of the Hell's Angels or January's centerfold girl, you just received your answer from God's word. Not that He does not love them as much as He loves you or that He does not have a plan and purpose for their lives. They are just not ready for a biblical marriage that would be in your best interest at this time. Therefore, most of our decisions can be based on what God tells us in His word. This is why it is so vitally important to put God's word in first place as we have greatly discussed. If you are going to be led by His word, you will have to listen and obey His word. The number one way God is going to lead you is through His word.

Other times, when God uses His word to lead you, you will be reading through it and come across a scripture. Then a situation or a decision that is needed will come up in our lives, and he will give you revelation knowledge about the decision that can even seem a little off topic of that scripture. The Holy Spirit will just kind of tap you on the shoulder, so to speak, and say, "Pay attention to this." Now, when it comes to something you do not have in the Bible, like "Should I take this job" or "Should I buy this car…" This is personal and specific to you and God's will for your life and He still has ways to lead you or answer a question.

Let's start where most people can understand. Some would call it your conscience. Think about what it feels like when you tell a bold-faced lie. How does that feel deep down in your heart when you do it? That is your spirit, by the Holy Spirit talking to you and saying, "This is wrong and a bad decision." But when we tell the truth, we get a comforting feeling and that is our conscience telling us, "This is good and the right decision." The world calls it our conscience, but that is because they do not really understand that it is our spirit where God inhabits.

God speaks to your spirit in this same manner through your conscience (spirit) when you are seeking His will in prayer, as described above. Even some religious people will call it your **soul** but that is also incorrect. Your soul is in the mental realm of your mind, will, and emotions. This is your spirit, the real you, where the Holy Spirit lives and communicates with you.

That is why sin is so devastating to us. It sears our conscience and cuts off all communications with our spirit. What we are doing is cutting off the only lines of communication we have with the Holy Spirit in the process. That is how the devil tries to destroy us. He tries to use sin to cut us off from our means of direct communication with God and to keep us from getting direct counterintelligence from God to make the correct decisions in our lives. It is a classic case of **divide and conquer**. It is his way of pulling us away from the authority and the strength we have in Christ so he can defeat us because he is powerless against us otherwise.

Also, it is sometimes an intuition that you just know something in your spirit that there is no way you could have known in your mind. Deep down, you just know it. It can also come from a desire. It says in God's word that He will *give us the desires of our hearts* (Psalm 37:4).

I used to think out of selfishness about that verse. That if I had a desire, God would give it to me because He loved me. While this is true, God is our father who loves to give His children gifts because He loves us. However, through the Holy Spirit giving me revelation knowledge about this verse, it also means something different that was awesomely cool. That God would put His will for our lives in our hearts as a **desire** within us to give us the desires of our hearts. So, God could give us the desires of our hearts and would help lead us to our destiny in the process, as well as give us the passion to pursue it. In both of these cases, it still has to line up with His word, and we still have to pray about it and listen to that still soft voice in our spirit because the devil cannot read our minds, but he can put thoughts in our minds.

For example, the devil could put a desire in you to drink a fifth of whiskey. This one would be obvious but some of them are not so obvious. The best way not to fall for this is just to try not to make snap decisions any more than you have to. Give yourself some time seeking guidance in God's word and seek direction using John 10:4–5—listen to that still, soft voice in your spirit, and just trust Him. It says in His word, *my sheep know my voice and a stranger they will not follow* (John 10:4–5).

Yes, we will still miss it sometimes, but the more we practice this, the easier it will become, and the better we will become at hearing it. As always, remember that God is your father; He knows when you are trying your best, and He is always looking for opportunities to provide an abundance of grace!

Kenneth E Hagin has written books, such as *How You Can Be Led by the Spirit of God* and a sermon series on CDs called *How to Train the Human Spirit*. These are a must-read if you truly want to fulfill the meaning of life while you are here on this earth. In this book, I am giving you a condensed version of how to be led by God's word and by the Holy Spirit. However, if you want more revelation knowledge about how to be led by the Spirit, I highly suggest you read or listen to these two books.

One of the things that I learned from the book *How You Can Be Led by the Spirit of God*, was to practice "instantly obeying the voice of your spirit."[13] Remember, learning how to hear God's voice is something that you practice getting better at. So, I just did what he said and started practicing it. Anytime I even felt like the Holy Spirit said something to me in my spirit, I instantly obeyed and did what He told me.

For, example, if I was watching a show with my family and felt in my spirit that I needed to pray about something or

---

13   "How to Train the Human Spirit. Adapted from How You Can Be Led by the Spirit of God: Legacy Edition.," Kenneth Hagin Ministries, accessed July 11, 2024, https://www.rhema.org/index.php?option=com_content&view=article&id=2502:how-to-train-the-human-spirit&catid=253:january-2016&Itemid=846.

someone, I would instantly get up, go to my room, and pray. It did not matter to me if I did not exactly know what I was praying for or how to pray for someone He put on my heart. I just did the best I could as an act of obedience. I may have only prayed for three minutes and then rejoined the family and finished watching the show with my family. However, what was important was that I was practicing instantly obeying the voice of my spirit and trying to at least go through the motions to try to do what God told me to do.

Another example of this is if God placed it on my heart to bless somebody with something like finances or my time (seed time and harvest). I would just do it. In that stage of learning, it was just more important that I acted upon it even if I was not efficient at it. The more you practice doing this, the clearer the Holy Spirit's voice will become to you. If God cannot trust us to act on these little things, how can we expect to receive the larger, more important things?

The Holy Spirit is speaking to our spirits constantly all day long. The Holy Spirit is connected to our spirits every bit as much as our minds are connected to our bodies. There is constant communication even if we are not hearing it. Many times, we hear it, but we do not realize it is the Holy Spirit speaking to us. We just think it is our thoughts. He is always speaking, so we just have to learn how to have our spiritual antennas tuned in to His frequency.

Right now, at this moment, where you are, there are hundreds of channels and frequencies broadcasting, but you cannot see or hear them. In the natural realm, all you need is a radio to dial to different frequencies to hear the different channels. In the spiritual realm, your spirit is the radio device the Holy Spirit uses (not your soul or mind).

We just have to train our spirits in how to dial into the frequency of the Holy Spirit's voice within us. The more we practice it, the more clearly we hear it so that we can hear it more often and more precisely. The only way to do this is practice. Most importantly, the more we practice it, the better we become at it. If I had not tried to keep this book short, I could have given you so many testimonies where the voice of the Holy Spirit saved my life and from bad situations.

When we look at our children and think that we could not even imagine loving someone as much as we do them, God loves us more than that, times one hundred. We are His children, and He loves us more than we can imagine, with an agape type of love that we cannot even comprehend or give in the flesh. God wants to communicate with us and have a personal, intimate relationship with us just like we do with our children. He has a perfect plan for our lives and wants to bless us beyond our wildest imagination. Only if we will try our best one day at a time to walk out His purpose and plan that He has for us, will we never be able to compare anything in the world to it. He does this through communicating through our spirits because He desires a close, intimate relationship with us for all eternity and thereafter. It is important to have an intimate relationship with God and to have consistent communication, like with any relationship. We do this through His word and fellowshipping with the Holy Spirit through our spirits, learning to hear His voice.

CHAPTER 16

Pay It Forward!

Once we learn how to operate in the Kingdom of God utilizing the *Five Simple Truths*, we should endeavor to share and train these truths with anybody who will listen. Most importantly, for our families and the people we love. For example, Elijah trained Elisha to be prepared to take up his mantle once he was gone. Elijah's last recorded miracle that completed his double portion anointing, which he requested from God, was even after he was dead (2 Kings 2:9–14). You see, Elijah asked Elisha what He could do for him before his time was done on this earth. Elisha said to have a double portion of the anointing of Elijah's spirit. Elijah said that was a hard thing to grant, but if Elisha saw him go to Heaven, he would be granted the request.

Once the day came and Elijah was taken up to Heaven, Elisha saw him go, and Elijah's staff fell down to earth. Then, Elisha immediately picked it up, and without skipping a beat, he took the staff, struck the Jordan River, and walked back over on dry ground just like Elijah did. Then, he went on to perform twice the recorded miracles that Elijah had while he was on this earth. Elisha's anointing was so strong that when he was dead, some Israelites who were burying a man were scared of some Moabite raiders, and quickly they threw the corpse into Elisha's tomb, and when it hit Elisha's bones, the man came back to life again (2 Kings 13:20–21). This should be our goal, to be an Elijah and train Elisha to pick up the mantle from things that we have learned.

I would like to briefly write directly to my fellow brothers in the Lord who are husbands and fathers. I cannot truly speak of what it is like or what God would expect of me as a godly wife and a mother because I truly have never been one. However, I am in awe of that wonderful, intricate, splendid being God created! True enough, in God's word, He did say that we were the head of the household. Except, that is not some kind of birthright or a gifted entitlement. He did not give us this commission so we could Lord it over them and run around thinking we are the boss of everything or treat them like our children. In fact, it is just the opposite. I know I may not win a popularity contest with this, but everything I wrote about in this book is our responsibility as husbands and fathers, and we will be held accountable.

We were commissioned by God to love our wives (and families) like Christ loves the Church. This commission was to be the spiritual leader of the household. We think we are supposed to be macho and protect our wives and families when the bad guy shows up. That is true; it is our responsibility, but that is only a fraction and the least of it. We are responsible for building the walls of protection around our families, which we have discussed so much about in this book.

The real bad guy we are commissioned to protect our families from is the devil who came to **kill, steal, and destroy** (John 10:10). More importantly, as a true leader, we are supposed to **lead**, which means to lead by example. Another aspect of our responsibility is that most of us do things in excess. We are out there working so hard and many hours to provide for our families and to give them the things that they need and the things we want them to have. And in the process, we become so driven, busy, and distracted that we sacrifice what is most important.

The most important thing that we could ever do, as husbands and fathers, is to learn how to be led by our spirits as well as operating in our authority. The Holy Spirit guides us to our destiny, which our families are a part of it. Also, He protects our families from the inevitable battles that the devil would rage against them. In the process of doing this, we are leading them to learn how to do it for their lives and their families, which they will eventually have one day.

I see in everyday life that this is all out of whack. I see men focusing on the temporal and leaving it to our wives to take our kids to church and be the spiritual leader while we are out there pursuing what we think is more important when it is really not. I can write about this because I have been that very same person, and it is my biggest regret to this day. So, all I am saying, my brothers, is that our commission as a leader in the spiritual realm is a thousand times more important than the physical one. Respectfully, let me finish out by saying that if we focus on our spiritual responsibility and build our relationship with God, as we have learned in this book, our physical goals and responsibilities will take care of themselves.

> *But seek ye first the kingdom of God, and his righteousness; and all these things shall be added unto you.*
>
> — Matthew 3:33 (KJV)

As far as wives and mothers are concerned, I truly am in awe of you. There are self-centered people in each gender. However, for the overwhelming majority, there is not another creature on this planet that is more nurturing than a mom and a wife, especially a mom—always putting their families, lives, and interests ahead of their own. They care about each intricate thing in their families lives. They do their best to ensure their children have the best clothes they can afford, their favorite food on the table and in their lunch boxes, etc. Moms do everything they can do to make sure that their children have an enjoyable childhood, from activities to all the latest technology and gadgets. Plus, they make sure their kids get a good education for their future. There is nothing more protective than a mom over her children. Hell knows no fury worse than a mother protecting her child, from the bully down the street to the mean teacher in the classroom.

But in your endeavor to do all these wonderful and selfless things you do for your family, just remember that all these things in the natural have a spiritual counterpart that is way more important because they are eternal. Sure, children need a good education in order to operate on this earth and try to better themselves in the natural world. However, being a born-again child of God and spiritually building them up are a thousand times more important. For them to spend eternity with their heavenly father (and you) in Heaven instead of somewhere else, we will just say it will be unpleasant without him (and you) for eternity.

Education may give them a little head start, but learning the things we have discussed in this book about who they are in Christ can give them way more success in this life and for eternity than an education ever could. Also, an education will never give them their meaning of life without pursuing the life that God planned for them. Remember, treat their spiritual nutrition with at least as much importance as their physical nutrition. Make sure that their spiritual education and nutrition are at least as equally important as their intellectual and physical ones because the devil will be the biggest bully they will ever encounter. He is way more than that bully down the street or that mean teacher could ever compare to or have a fraction of the impact on their lives as he can. However, with everything that has been outlined in this book, you will have plenty of weapons in your arsenal to protect your children and train them to protect themselves and their families in the future.

This particular chapter was very difficult for me to write because, in the process, I feel like the biggest hypocrite on this planet. I must confess that I failed miserably in this department. My failure in this area is the single biggest regret in my life. This chapter is what I meant in the opening statement where hopefully this book would be like getting a letter from your future self. The time we have with our children is so precious, but it truly is like a flash of time. It seems like you start off changing diapers, and you blink your eyes, and you are helping them change the tire on their car. The time you have with your children is short, so make sure to equip them in all areas of their lives so that they can fulfill the meaning of their life.

Originally, the intended purpose of this book was for my children, grandchildren, and even great, great-grandchildren whom I may never even have a chance to meet. As well as family, friends, and people God put across my path. I felt that I could never expect them to do all the studying I have done for the last thirty-five years. So, I took everything that I learned and condensed it down for them with the most important things of every aspect of life for them. I myself had never come across a book that compiled all the vital things in a condensed version. I wanted something in my hands that I could give to someone I love so that I could give them more information in one small book than study hundreds like I did. I felt I might have the chance to encourage them to at least read this one small book for no other reason than to get me off their backs so I would leave them alone… LOL. In the name of Jesus, I pray this book will be a tool in your hands as well.

CHAPTER 17

Executing the Meaning of Life

I am not saying that the things that I have tried to convey in this book as being complicated. In fact, what I am saying is just the opposite. I am just a simple man with average intelligence who has grabbed ahold of some simple truths from God's word and has sought out mentors like Kenneth E Hagin, Andrew Womack, and many others. *The Five Simple Truths* from God's word have been at least enough to make me dangerous for the kingdom of darkness. I just tried my best to convey these simple truths that I have learned to you.

I believe most people are like me; if it is complicated, we are probably never going to put it into practice. What good is a weapon if you do not know how to use it? My goal was to keep this book as short as possible with as much simple executable information to fulfill the meaning of your life and how to protect your family and your life in the process. In this book, we have covered *The Meaning of Life*, *The Five Simple Truths*, and *The Five-Step Battle Plan,* and we exposed the devil's weapons that he tries to use against them. Then, with these truths, we can live an extremely satisfying and victorious life on this earth. If you only took this book and read it over and over again until these truths were deeply embedded in your spirit, you could live this life on earth in complete victory in every battle and have a life full of joy, peace, prosperity, and full of God's glory!

God gave us free will, and the choice is ours to make. We can choose Jesus, who said, *"I have come so that they [you] may have life, and have it abundantly"* (John 10:10 NASB), or we can choose the devil, who is here to **kill, steal, and destroy**. There is no middle ground; we choose one or the other—and making no choice at all defaults to the latter.

So, *The Meaning of Life* boils down to this. Do you want to spend your life trying to fulfill the desires of the flesh… allowing the devil to be constantly shoving counterfeits down your throat instead of receiving all the miraculous God has prepared for you… let the devil deceive you and sidetrack you from your purpose and the plans God has for you… and fill us with fear, anxiety, hopelessness, and failures, and empty as a bucket, broken, sick, and disgusted… and trying to chase after and fill a bucket that has no bottom to it… then, let the devil **kill, steal, and destroy** your life, joy, peace, confidence, strength, success, soul, body, and your purpose… ultimately, try to bring us down into an entity with him that we will just say, "It will be unpleasant" for eternity? Hell was not created for a child of God, and Jesus paid the ultimate sacrifice so that it would not be.

Alternatively, do we want a close personal relationship with God… Operate in the spiritual realm as a spirit being where miracles exist through faith… by renewing our minds with the word of God of who we are in Christ and what He has done for us by His death, burial, and resurrection. That allows us to take authority over the kingdom of darkness in the name of

Jesus against anything the devil would try to harm us with or steal from us.

So, just simply try your best one day at a time to navigate your way in life through Him and by His strength, power, and wisdom to achieve the unimaginable awesome plan He has for your life here on earth, as well as eternity. God will equip us to face and live this life here fearlessly and courageously and achieve a purposeful, meaningful, and satisfying life. It is not just for success and joy on this earth but also to be prepared for the unimaginable and euphoric eternity with God. Jesus loves us so much that He died for us so that we can share eternity with Him. Also, it provides a **hedge of protection** around our children and us as we learn who we are in Christ and all that Jesus paid for at the cross. Remember, even Job had a **hedge of protection** at one point until he, not God, lowered it with **seed time and harvest** of his words of fear, lack of faith, and trust in God. Plus, this hedge of protection is not only for us but also for our family, to be able to protect everything we love and care about in this world.

So, where do you go from here? How do you even start a new positive path in life with our heavenly father? It is really up to you. You have to set goals for yourself; no one can do that for you. Only you know your time, schedule, and motivation. When I first started reading who I really was in Christ, I became so hungry for God's word I could not get enough and still cannot. Let me break this up into two categories of people.

Let's start with someone who has already been a Christian for a while and at least has a basic foundation of the word of God. If you just highlight the important parts of this book that spoke to you and feed on them until they become yours, you could be 10 feet tall and bulletproof in a very short period of time (along with practicing it). This is because there is nothing in this book that I would deem complicated by any means.

Faith is simple; man has made it complicated. I am sure you would be a lot like I was. It is not that I had not read these things. It is just that I did not have complete revelation knowledge of these things that I had already read.

Most importantly, be sure to remain in the word of God on a consistent and regular basis and build your spiritual knowledge through revelation knowledge by the Holy Spirit. Sometimes, it is also good to just start from scratch, and you can follow my suggestion next for more of a new believer if you are truly hungry for God's word and His promises. Then, live a life of victory in all areas of your life. Also, it does not matter how old you are, God can and will take you from where you are at this very moment.

For more of a new believer here is what I suggest. I would suggest setting an obtainable goal to get started. If you start off with something steady and obtainable for a while, you will find that naturally, you will become more hungry and more excited about the word of God. Then, it will no longer be some kind of goal but something you will naturally be hungry for, and it will no longer be a scheduled activity out of self-discipline to live and have a better rewarding life. I would suggest the following…

ONE…

It would be best to be in God's word, renewing your mind in some form every day to build yourself up and grow spiritually.

At least, find time a few times a week to read through the books in the New Testament. Start with the book of Matthew, end with the book of Jude, and then start back at Matthew again.

If you have a study Bible, I would suggest having a highlighter and highlight anything that jumps out at you. That is the Holy Spirit speaking to you trying to give you revelation knowledge. I would avoid the book of Revelation to start. It is mainly about the future, and your first priority is your present. The New Testament is really who we are in Christ and is the most important foundation to get started. Also, you can watch YouTube and listen to teachings from your computer or cell phone.

If I am driving and it is more than a 15-minute trip, there is never a time I do not have some kind of teaching to feed on while I am driving. If we can learn how to take advantage of times that are kind of wasted time anyway, we can grow really fast this way, even if we do not have a lot of time. I still actively do this on a daily basis. I look forward to nighttime to be able to put on a teaching beside my bed to feed on as I am going to sleep. It is kind of like white noise till I go to sleep. Charisbiblecollege.org has thousands of hours of free teaching you can find on their website. It is really a great place if you need healing. They have yearly healing school conferences with many speakers. You can go to the website and listen to years' worth of these archived teachings.

Andrew Wommack is a gifted teacher and explains deep spiritual truths that a third-grader could understand. He has a ton of free stuff on YouTube as well. The four-part series we mentioned earlier, *Harnessing Your Emotions,* is a must! Also, there is *You Already Got It* and *Spirit, Soul and Body*. You really need to listen to these.

Kenneth E. Hagin is who I would consider my spiritual father in the beginning. His book *The Believers Authority* is also an absolute must-read. I am pretty sure it is a four-part series that you can also find on YouTube, but the book is much better to study.

My goal in this book was to keep everything short and condensed so that it would be user-friendly. However, if you are truly sincere about being led by your spirit for your destiny, then you truly must read and study the book *How You Be Led by the Spirit of God and the sermon series on CD's, how to Train the Human Spirit* by Kenneth E. Hagin mentioned earlier. Also, you can find on YouTube for free. I do not think there is a full gospel preacher on this earth today who has not read and learned from these two books by him. They truly are a must read for your foundation. Plus, he has a ton of stuff on YouTube even though he has gone to be with the Lord. He truly was the spiritual leader for most of the great pastors that we have that are preaching the full gospel of Jesus Christ today. There are many others I could recommend but these are more than enough to get you started. I listed all these books and a few others at the end of this book under study materials. If you study all these on the list, you would be able to school must pastors... LOL.

Each time before you start reading God's word, ask Him to speak to you through His word and make Himself real to you. Also, remember James 1:5 as you endeavor to follow God's will for your life.

I have included the two prayers out of the book of Ephesians that Paul prayed for the Church of emphasis, and you should pray them every time before you start reading the word. I learned this from Kenneth E. Hagin. He said he prayed this prayer for himself for thirty days and felt he learned more in those thirty days than he had in the thirty years prior because of revelation knowledge versus just head knowledge.

The main goal of the prayers that I combined and put in personal pronouns and included them at the end of this book so that you can pray them for yourself, and the first part of the prayer is for revelation knowledge. You can read the Bible and find a lot of truths and direction. The Bible is not just a book. It is spiritually alive and needs revelation knowledge to really come alive in your life. So, I would suggest reading the Ephesians prayer for yourself each time before reading the word.

I also included the *Psalm 91 Prayer* that I copied using personal pronouns to declare it over your family and yourself. I have another son who is still alive today because of this prayer over him, but that is another testimony and book in itself. It is also an intricate prayer that is preparation for a battle before the enemy shows up at your gate, where it comes to you and your family. It helps you build your wall and hedge of protection, which we discussed so much in this book.

This prayer helps you to have revelation knowledge that you are in God's protection if you are trusting Him to do so based on His promise to you in His word by **faith**. It guards you against the devil's raging war in your mind, who is trying to flood you with fear, anxiety, and unbelief.

Then, while I was at it, I included a copy of the *Seven Steps to Answered Prayer* that I wrote a long time ago. It is to be used as a kind of a short, condensed cheat sheet when you are in the middle of a battle and you need an answered prayer. It is just another weapon in your arsenal to strengthen you against the battle that the devil rages against you.

TWO...

We should pray every day, and I recommend that you do so. If you can, start with or at least try to spend half an hour of fellowshipping time with Him. Here again, you can use wasted time like driving to talk to Him and just hang out with Him. Also, anytime you feel lonely, fearful, or anxious, it would be a great time to talk to God.

There are no drugs on the market that compare to spending time with the Holy Spirit. He just sucks that nasty junk like fear, anxiety, and low self-esteem the world puts on us right out of us. What I do is save a couple of what they call *soaking music* to my favorites on YouTube on my phone. Most of them are advertised for things like falling asleep or mental healing. Also, I guess they work for that purpose because many times before I am done praying, I end up falling asleep… LOL. But that is ok, just remember God is your father, and what Father would be upset if His child fell asleep in His arms? Just something soothing and instrumental playing softly in the background while you are praying with no words that your mind could miss direct. It just helps me set the worship atmosphere.

Remember, in the process, God does not care about all that formality in prayer. Just start with praise, think about things that you are grateful for in your life, and thank Him for it. The fact that you are His child and all He has provided for you is enough to praise Him for hours. So, praise Him for all that you have discovered that belongs to you, that you learned from the *Five Simple Truths* concerning who you are and what He has done for you as His child. Also, this is part of renewing your mind and building up your spiritual armor. Praise Him for your **hedge of protection** that He has provided by who you are in Christ and the Psalm 91 prayer. As you are praising Him for these things, you are simultaneously operating in **seed time and harvest** by your words being spoken as a seed for them. This is fortifying the walls around you and your family 101. In Psalms, it says in God's word that He inhabits the *praises of His people.*

> *But thou art holy, O thou that inhabitest the praises of Israel.*
>
> — Psalm 22:3 (KJV)

No father wants to be treated like Santa Claus. That does not mean we should not ask for things; that is what He is there for. Just do not make that the priority; let fellowship be the priority. Prayer is fellowship with God, not a wish list. Remember, we do not have to pray about things He has already promised us in His word. We do not have any reason to treat God like Santa Claus or waste His valuable fellowship time with Him, asking Him to give us something He has already given us. That is up to us to find that out in God's word and declare and receive it based on God's word and His promises by our **faith**, which we have discussed so much in this book. Then it becomes part of praise and worship time instead. However, that is still what He is there for. I may be standing on God's word and His promises about a healing, but I am still going to pray about it with Him while I am praising Him for it in the process.

As discussed earlier, praise and worship remove unbelief from our faith and usher in joy and peace, which is the opposite of fear, worry, and unbelief. As I am praising Him for my healing, I am operating in seed time and harvest at the same time. This is part of praise and worship, thanking Him for these things you declared based on His word and His promises. When you are praising Him for these things with your words, that is **seed time and harvest** in operation at the same time. Ask Him for the opportunity to do something for the Kingdom of God that day.

I do not have a specific scripture and verse for this, but if I do have concerns or fears that are creeping in on me and I do not have an answer at that moment, I pray to Him in silence or in the spirit over these issues. I know it seems crazy, but I do not want my enemy to hear things like this coming out of my mouth as God works with me on them. I do not want them to be potential seeds that are planted with my words out loud with my mouth into the earth.

So, just talk to Him. He is like a friend that you can confide in about anything. You do not have to put on a fake persona with Him because He already knows every thought in your mind. You cannot hide anything, but that is what is so great about it. That just means you do not have to try to hide anything because you cannot, anyway. You can be yourself and say whatever is in your heart. Like talking to a psychiatrist, the only difference is this one loves you beyond comprehension and can actually transform, heal, and empower you. Then just talk to Him, ask Him questions, ask Him to show you His will for your life, for that day. Ask Him to give you eyes to see and ears to hear His voice in your spirit, and ask Him for revelation knowledge of His word.

THREE...

As I mentioned earlier, you could incorporate reading and studying this book. It truly is a condensed version of a lot of revelation knowledge that God has given me through His word and some great mentors. This is what you could call compounded revelation knowledge that you can use as kind of a shortcut while you are building your own relationship and foundation of revelation knowledge. And even shorter than that, like I said before, at least take the *Five Simple Truths* and the things that devour them and read them over and over again until they are embedded in your spirit!

My best advice is what I have learned to do personally with any book, including the Bible, which is I would read it once, and if I received any revelation knowledge from it, it would be worth reading again. We only retain about 2% at best of what we read, and if we learned anything at all, then it means we missed a lot. On the second time, I will take my highlighter and highlight everything that spoke to me from the first read, plus whatever I picked up the second time. If I was still receiving revelation knowledge I would read it a third time, and so on. If it was a good book, by then, I would have yellow highlights all over the place. Then I would just go back and feed (devour), declare those yellow highlighted truths until that revelation knowledge was transferred to me and embedded in my spirit. Some of the foundational books I mentioned above looked like they had been dropped in lemonade and used for a broom by the time I was done with them…LOL. This is how you meditate on God's word and how you get transformed by the renewing of your mind (change your mindset).

FOUR…

Do something daily toward your future. Start practicing hearing God's voice and instantly obeying the voice of your spirit so you can follow God's plan for your life. Avoid traps that the devil would place in front of you, and actively build your walls of protection around your family and you as discussed earlier.

Slowly start weeding things out of your life that are holding you back or harmful to your spirit, soul, and body. Remember what Jordan B. Peterson suggested: just sit on the side of your bed and ask yourself what is holding you back. God built and designed you to do exciting and wonderful things on this earth while you are here… go after them and achieve them as He proposed you to do!

My biggest desire is for you to pursue this extraordinary journey God has planned for your life. Also, by walking through this life in the spiritual realm as a spiritual being and operating in the Kingdom of God where miracles exist, we can pull them into the natural realm. Thereby, live in complete victory and authority in this life in the process and especially the euphoric eternity that is beyond your wildest dreams and imaginations.

I did my best to give you short yet powerful practical ways to achieve the meaning of your life while on this earth. I tried my best to stay focused on all the information that was the most vital to help you build your revelation knowledge of who you are in Christ and all that He has done and purchased for you at the cross. Also, I showed you how to build your wall of protection around your family and you. One thing in this book that is driven home many times is the fact that we have to be so saturated with the word of God and His promises that we are well prepared for any attack of the devil long before He shows up. More importantly, keep him away from our gates from the beginning.

Almost every sentence in this book came from some form of revelation knowledge from God's word. So, if you did nothing else but read this book once a week, you could be years ahead in your revelation knowledge in a short period of time. What is awesome is that in the process, the Holy Spirit will be flooding your spirit with your own revelation knowledge in His word.

There is a big misconception about Heaven, thinking you are going to be flying around in diapers with a harp singing "Praise the Lord" for eternity. That is so ridiculous! I have read and researched a lot of resource materials, books, and podcasts of testimonies about Heaven. If we truly comprehended what it was like, we would almost be worthless on this earth because all we want to do is be there. Everything on this earth would fail in comparison. In every near-death experience about Heaven that I researched, the individual never wanted to come back to Earth because it was so awesome there. That is why this life is so important. It has a lot to do with what we will be doing in Heaven personally once we arrive there one day. Just try to keep in mind that we are only on this earth for a moment in comparison, but we will be in Heaven with Him for eternity.

If you are not a child of God who has been born again and washed in the blood of the Lord Jesus Christ for the remission of sin, let me encourage you to do so today. Everything in God's word and in this book is what Jesus, our Messiah, died on the cross to give you. Becoming a born-again child of God is the easiest thing to do on this planet. You cannot work your way into Heaven. You never can be good enough on your own living by the old law. It is a free gift from God that is given to us through grace by the ultimate sacrifice of the blood of the Lord Jesus Christ. All you have to do is pray the simple *Salvation Prayer* below. There are many ways you could ask but it covers everything necessary. All that matters is if you meant it from your heart, you are now a born-again child of God. Hallelujah! Glory to God!

It is that easy because God made it that easy for you by His grace… not works! God loved you so much that He sacrificed His son just for you!

THE SALVATION PRAYER

Jesus,

I believe You are the Son of God, Who was sacrificed as prophesied for me and rose again and paid for all my sins on the cross. Forgive me of my sins. I accept You as my Lord and Savior and ask You to come and live in my heart. I thank you that You are now my lord.

SEVEN STEPS TO AN ANSWERED PRAYER

1. Forgive anyone that has wronged you in any way. Unforgiveness is probably the number one prayer blocker. Jesus will forgive you for anything, and we must do the same. If you have a problem in this area just start praying for that person till you believe it. Remember, Jesus died for their mistakes just as He did for yours. He loves them just like He does you. They just yielded to the wrong spirit when they sinned against you just like you do when you sin against God. Is there really a grudge so important to you that it is worth blocking all your prayers and blessings? For the cheap cost of a petty grudge, they control your life and prayers. This is a trap from the devil. Who in this situation has the greater loss? Is it really worth it? Just pray for them once and for all, let it go, and then leave it between them and God. Then, by **faith**, you release the promises in God's word that He has already paid for and has given you through **seed time and harvest**.
2. Find promises in God's word that stand behind what you are praying. Find at least three

scriptures that promise you what you are asking God for and bring them before Him when you pray as the basis of what you are standing on. God said with two or three witnesses, every word will be established.

3. Ask God in faith, nothing wavering (void of unbelief). Like God, we are to call things that are not as though they are based on God's word and His promises that He has already given us.
4. Do not tolerate a thought that is contrary to what you are praying for based on God's word. When doubt, fear, worry, and unbelief come, doubt the devil's doubt, not God's word and promises. Should it not be easier for a child of God to doubt the devil's lies than God's word and His promises? Just start praising God for your answered prayer when doubt creeps in. Remember, if you are basing your answered prayer on the five physical senses, then it will not work because you are not applying God's word correctly. You are operating in the physical realm based on feelings, which is just the opposite of faith. Faith is the only thing that unlocks God's word and promises. For example, let's say you are praying for healing, and one day you feel better, and you say, "My prayers are being answered." Then, the next day, you do not feel as good and you say, "That the prayers are not." That is a trap from the devil to trick you back into the physical realm, where he will defeat you **every** time. So,

until you have the complete manifestation of your promised healing, base your confession only on God's word and not on feelings, good or bad. This works for any promise you have in God's word.

5. Simply put, base your faith on God's word and His promises alone and **nothing** else. Put God's word in first place.
6. Count the thing done. If you pray for something seven times, you have prayed six times in unbelief. Remember, getting your prayers answered is not as much as getting God to act on your behalf. It is us receiving what Jesus paid for and what God has already **promised** in **His word**. Again, like healing, God has already promised it, and Jesus has already died and paid for it with the stripes on His back. *"By Whose [His] stripes, ye were healed"* (2 Peter 2:4 KJV), which is past tense. It is up to **us** just to receive the healing that God has already promised, and Jesus has **already** for it the same as He did for our salvation. He does not have to come back and take stripes on His back every time we need healing, no more than He has to come back to die on the cross every time for someone to get saved. All we have to do is receive our salvation in faith by standing on God's word for what He has already done. So, is it God's fault if we do not receive salvation? **No**, it is up to us to **receive** the salvation that He has already paid

for and promised in His word. Everything that God has promised in His word works the same way—activating it by asking in **faith** based on God's word that promises it and confessing and standing in faith in His word. *"If thou canst believe all things are possible"* (Mark 9:23 KJV). Who has action in this verse? Us! We have to believe, which means **faith**. So, if we have trouble getting our prayers answered, we do not have a God problem; we have a faith problem by allowing the devil to attach unbelief to it. Many children of God are waiting around for God to do something, but it is Him who is doing the waiting. He has already done His part and given us His word and promises. It is up to us to receive His promises based on His word by following these seven steps that are based on God's word. Build your faith from God's word on what you are believing for from God's word and **receive** it. Want more faith, *"faith comeith by hearing, hearing by the word of God"* (Romans 10:17 KJV)!

7. Give God the glory now; faith is now. If it is not now, then it is not faith; it is hope. God never promised our prayers would be answered by hope, only faith. When Jesus prayed for Lazarus, He was still outside the tomb, and He thanked (or praised) God. He **had** (past tense) heard Him, but he was still dead in the natural. It was later, **after** they removed the wall from the

tomb opening and Jesus entered, that His prayer was manifested. That was Jesus showing us how prayer and faith work. He was operating in seed time and harvest with His words and for what He believed. You may say, "Well, that was Jesus." However, Peter did the same thing, and he did it the same way, and so can we. God said He was no respecter of persons. If He will do it for Peter, He will do it for us if we follow the same steps as they did, operating in faith. Jesus said, *"The works that I do shall he [you] do also; and even greater works than these shall he [you] do; because I go unto my Father"* (John 14:12 KJV). Once prayed for, stop praying and start praising Him for it every day and every time doubt sneaks in. When doubt comes, that is our queue to start praising God for our answered (past tense) prayer. And you keep praising Him till that doubt (devil) leaves you. *"Resist the devil and he will flee from you,"* (James 4:7 NIV). This usually does not take more than 1 to 2 minutes, but we do have to resist the devil on our part before we let our emotions get out of control. This does two things: turbo charges your faith back in line with God's word and His promises and puts the devil running from you like a scolded dog!

Now, act as though you have already received it. Start enjoying the blessing in your spirit now; that is up to us, not God. If we have done 1–7, it is ours now (a Christian walks by faith and not by sight). God cannot lie, and He said you can have what you say—Mark 11:23.

> *If you truly believe you have received (that is how faith works), would you not have joy now? Do you want God to have joy? Do you want God to have pleasure in you? But without faith it is impossible to please him [God].*
>
> — Hebrews 11:16 (KJV)

THE EPHESIANS PRAYER FOR REVELATION KNOWLEDGE

I pray that God, the glorious Father of my Lord Jesus Christ, will give me wisdom to see clearly and really understand who Christ is and all He has done for me. I pray that my heart will be flooded with light so that I can see something of the future You have called me to share. I pray and realize that God has been made rich because we, who are Christ, have been given to you. I pray that I will begin to understand how incredibly great Your power is to help those who believe in You. It is that same mighty power that raised Christ from the dead and seated Him in the place of honor at God's right hand in Heaven far, far above any other king, ruler, dictator, or leader.

Yes, His honor is far more glorious than that of anyone else in the world or the world to come, and God has put all things under His feet and made Him the supreme head of the church, which is His body, filled with Himself, the author and giver of everything everywhere… and lifted me up from the grave into glory along with Christ, where I now sit with

Him in the heavenly realm, all because of what Christ Jesus did.

When I think of the wisdom and scope of Your plan, I fall down on my knees and pray to the father of the great family of God; some of them are already in Heaven, and some down here on Earth. That out of Your glorious, unlimited resources, You will give me the mighty inner strengthening of the Holy Spirit.

I pray that Christ will be more and more at home in my heart, living within me as I trust in You. May my roots go down deep into the soil of God's marvelous love. And may I be able to feel and understand as all God's children should, how wide, how long, how deep, and how high Your love really is. And to experience this love for myself though it is so great that I will never see the end of it or fully know or understand it. And, so, at least, I will be filled with God Himself.

Now glory be to God, who, by Your mighty power at work within me, is able to do far more than I would ever dare ask or even dream of, infinitely, beyond my highest prayers, desires, thoughts, or hopes. May You be giving glory forever and ever through endless ages because of Your master plan of salvation for the Church through Jesus Christ.

— Adapted from Ephesians 1–3

PSALM 91 PRAYER

I live within the shadow of the almighty, sheltered by the God of all gods. This I declare that You alone are my refuge and my place of safety; You are my God, and I TRUST You!

For You rescue me from every trap and protect me from "the fatal plague."

You shield me with Your wings; they will shelter me.

Your faithful promises are my armor.

Now I don't have to be afraid of the dark anymore, nor fear the dangers of the day,

nor dread the plagues of darkness nor disasters in the morning.

Though a thousand fall at my side, though ten thousand are dying around me, the evil will not touch me.

I will see how the wicked are punished, but I will not share in it, for You are my refuge.

I choose the God above all gods to shelter me. How then can evil overtake me or any plague come near?

For You order Your angels to protect me wherever I go.

They will steady me with their hands to keep me from stumbling against the rocks on the trail.

I can safely meet a lion or step on a poisonous snake; yes, I even trample them beneath my feet.

For You, Lord says.

Because He loves me, I will rescue Him and honor Him; I will make Him great because He TRUSTS in my name. When He calls on me, I will answer; I will be with Him in trouble and rescue Him and honor Him. I will satisfy Him with a FULL life and give Him my salvation.

— Adapted from Psalm 91

SUGGESTED STUDY RESOURCE MATERIALS

KENNETH E. HAGIN

- *How You Can Be Led by Your Spirit*
- *How to Train the Human Spirit* (CD sermon series)
- *The Believer's Authority*
- *Mountain Moving Faith*
- *Redeemed from the Curse of the Law*
- *Healing Classics* (6 CD sermon series)

ANDREW WOMMACK

- *Harnessing Your Emotions*
- *Spirit, Soul, and Body*
- *You've Already Got It*
- *The Power of Imagination*
- *A Better Way to Pray*

F. F. BOSWORTH

- *Christ the Healer*

I could give you many others, but this is more than enough for now to get started. They will lead you to many others by the Holy Spirit. Most of these materials can be found on YouTube.

REFERENCES

"Grace." 2024. Oxford English Dictionary. 2024. https://www.oed.com/dictionary/grace_n.

Hagin, Kenneth E. 1986. *The Believer's Authority*. 2nd edition. Faith Library Publications.

"How to Train the Human Spirit. Adapted from How You Can Be Led by the Spirit of God: Legacy Edition." n.d. Kenneth Hagin Ministries. Accessed July 11, 2024. https://www.rhema.org/index.php?option=com_content&view=article&id=2502:how-to-train-the-human-spirit&catid=253:january-2016&Itemid=846.

"Meditate." n.d. The Oxford Pocket Dictionary of Current English. Encyclopedia.Com. Accessed June 17, 2024. https://www.encyclopedia.com/humanities/dictionaries-thesauruses-pictures-and-press-releases/meditate-0.

"Reign." 2024. Merriam-Webster Online Dictionary. Merriam-Webster, Incorporated. July 3, 2024. https://www.merriam-webster.com/dictionary/reign.

Rev. Kenneth E. Hagin. 1985. *Healing Classics*. Faith Library Publications.

Rik. 2022. "What Does the Bible Say about Changes in Your Life?" *Self Growth Resources* (blog). November 2, 2022. https://selfgrowthresources.com/what-does-the-bible-say-about-changes-in-your-life/.

Sanders, Bohdi. 2016. "Project Strength to Avoid Conflict ~ Bohdi Sanders." *The Wisdom Warrior* (blog). February 17, 2016. https://thewisdomwarrior.com/2016/02/17/project-strength-to-avoid-conflict/.

Savchuk, Vladimir. 2021. "7 Steps to Renew Your Mind." Vladimir Savchuk Ministries. January 17, 2021. https://pastorvlad.org/mindrenewal/.

Shapiro, Ben. 2019. *Facts Don't Care about Your Feelings*. Creators Publishing.

"Startling Evidence for Noah's Flood." 2024. Answers in Genesis. 2024. https://answersingenesis.org/geology/grand-canyon-facts/startling-evidence-for-noahs-flood/.

"Why Did Jesus Say, 'Do Not Fear; Only Believe' to the Ruler of the Synagogue (Mark 5:36)?" 2023. GotQuestions.Org. 2023. https://www.gotquestions.org/do-not-fear-only-believe.html.

Wikipedia Contributors. 2024. "The Enemy of My Enemy Is My Friend." In *Wikipedia, The Free Encyclopedia*. https://en.wikipedia.org/w/index.php?title=The_enemy_of_my_enemy_is_my_friend&oldid=1229288595.

ABOUT THE AUTHOR

At the age of 62, I look back on my life and realize just how intricate God was in every stage of my life. He led me through each stage to prepare me for the next. From age 21 until I was 36, I spent most of my career in sales. Through this, I had abundant opportunities to receive a lot of wonderful training that would highly shape the future of my life. The training that influenced me was from people like Norman Vincent Peale, Zig Ziggler, and many others. This type of training was about learning how to be successful, learn human psychology, and how to think positively.

However, the Holy Spirit would later transform it in a completely different direction. In my mid-thirties, I graduated from Rhema Correspondent Bible Training College in Broken Arrow, OK. In the process of incorporating human psychology and religion, it gave me a unique perspective on how to operate in the Kingdom of God through faith. Since 2000, I have been an independent business owner. God has blessed me beyond my wildest imagination through the principles and the promises in His word and operating in faith.

Printed in the USA
CPSIA information can be obtained
at www.ICGtesting.com
CBHW052000311024
16597CB00018B/114